The Road to Glen Spean

The Road to Glen Spean

Christina Hall

Birlinn

First published in 2005 by
Birlinn Limited
West Newington House
10 Newington Road
Edinburgh EH9 1QS

www.birlinn.co.uk

British Library Cataloguing-in-Publication Data
A catalogue record for this book is available from the
British Library

Typeset by Textype, Cambridge
Printed and bound by Nørhaven Paperback A/S, Viborg

For Rose Ellen and Meredith,
Tom and Andy

Tilleadh Alick

Gur dorcha neul-bhreac than a speuran
A ghaoth mar phuinnsean, fuar is geur oirnn
Tha 'Triath nan Eilean' ti'nn gu cala
Le oigear eileanach nach gluais.

Luchd caoidh na seasamh teann ri'n gualainn
Air cidhe samhach tursach truaghail
Air monadh Choinnich tha na feidh
Gun ghluasad, gun eibh nan luib.

Cha chuir a fuachd a phiob gu samhchair
Do chumha ceolmhor Aonaghais cuir failte
Air Alick 'se tilleadh air ais don'n aite
Far na thar' e a cheud anail.

Tha'n t-eilein suaint ime fhein 'sa chairdean
Caite faigh me e, an d'rinn e m'fhagail?
The e 'san oiteag, an gailinn a gheamhraidh
An osna na gainmhich gun cluinn me e fhathast.
Se an iolair th'air iteig os cionn na Beinn Mhoir
Se a grian air a Bharp aluinn dannsail mar or
Ann an cumha na curracaic gun cluinn mi a cheol
Ann an laighe na greine tha e dearrsadh le gloir
Ann an laighe na greine tha e dearrsadh le gloir.

Alick's Return

The sky above is mottled
And the air as cold as poison
The Lord of the Isles returns
With a fallen son.

And the little band of mourners
Stand silent by the pier side
And the deer stand silent
On Coinneach's slopes.

Angus too defies the coldness
To play a sad lament
As Alick, he returns once more
To where he first began.

For he and his are the island
So where shall I find him?
He is in the tempest's roar
And in the sighing sand.
He's the eagle that hovers over o'er Ben Mor
The sunlight dancing on Barp
In the lapwing's cry in machair skies
And in the setting sun
The glowing, setting sun.

Cliff Crook, 2003

Chapter One

'WELL WELL, IT IS YOURSELF, MRS HALL! Would you hold my pipe while I give Skip another wee drop . . . and show him the road and the miles to Dundee.' The end of the sentence was sung lustily in a reedy though not unpleasant voice belonging to one James MacPherson, our landlord in Benbecula. He was sitting on the floor of our shared kitchen at midnight, with a can of beer in his right hand and his left arm round the neck of Skip, our Border Collie who was trying to dodge the smoke from James's pipe and lick the pattern off a suspiciously frothy saucer at the same time. I had been fast asleep when Annabel, James's sister, had knocked on our bedroom door in a highly nervous state, and asked if one of us would go and investigate the strange noises coming from the kitchen. My fairly new husband who had done a hard day's work was dead to the world, and as the only strange noises I could hear were a rousing chorus of 'The Road to Dundee' accompanied by the occasional 'Woo woo' from Skip I knew that my first home as a new bride was not in any danger from burglars.

I had left my parents' croft in Kilpheder, on the island of South Uist, and was now living on the neighbouring island of Benbecula; the long journey from Glendale, where I had been teaching a few weeks before this musical interruption of my night's sleep, towards beautiful Glen Spean in Roy Bridge where I now write this, had begun.

To go from South Uist to Roy Bridge at present usually takes a day whichever way you do it. The ferry and bus or car journey taking the Lochmaddy–Uig–Kyle–Fort Augustus–Spean Bridge route to Roy Bridge, with the usual built-in delays is tedious and time consuming. In my case my travels took thirty-nine years and covered 45,000 miles. I don't include distances covered for holidays in this. The miles I count were travelled complete with husband, children, all household effects and sometimes a dog or two on the way to new homes. Were I to add the total mileage I clocked up between then and now inclusive of pleasure trips I'd come to the conclusion that if I was a secondhand car I would not buy myself.

The pattern of my life up to the date of my marriage had not been what you'd expect for a child growing up on an island croft and many people who have read about it have called some of it harrowing, but it has probably given me my lifelong Micawber-like blind faith that things will always turn out for the best, especially if I give them a shove from time to time.

As a single person I had never really had much of a say in where I was going to live. My parents had handed me over to my aunts to bring up when I was four and a half, as they themselves already had more than enough children to cope with, and were running out of beds. So I lived with the two, very strict, middle-aged ladies, one a teacher and the other her housekeeper on the Hebridean islands of Benbecula and Barra, for my primary school years. The need to finish my education meant a return to Uist, then on to Fort William, and Glasgow for teacher training. When completed I returned to Uist to teach in Glendale, Daliburgh and Glendale again, with a short period in Glasgow in between. I had plans to emigrate to Canada but fate intervened and I married a soldier instead. Now I was beginning to find out that I would not have any fixed home or even country of permanent abode for many years to come.

That was the way of it with the women of my generation born just before the start of the Second World War. In childhood you followed a pattern of life laid out for you by your parents. In my own case school and college were followed by graduation into an adult life of work where you could find it, and be glad of it. There was no such thing as a gap year. If you took a year off during your studies it meant only one thing . . . you had failed your exams and could certainly not afford to spend any time travelling round the world studying the rainforests. You had to try and find another way into a course of studies, or accept some unskilled job that would earn you a living. If and when you got married, you gave up your independence and concentrated on whatever would make life as comfortable as possible for your family unit. As a way of life it would certainly drive some of the modern generation of highly motiv- ated career-minded women to sneer at the 'exploitation' we suffered. Indeed, some people of my own age shud- der when I tell them that this is my twenty-second home. However I can say, hand on heart, that were I given the chance to start again I would not change a minute of it.

Before I met Colin, my husband, I had given little thought to the subject of life as part of a married couple, other than the usual girlhood vision of myself one day, in a dim and distant future, wearing the white dress surrounded by bridesmaids fluttering all over the place, a big party with a cake and a shadowy figure repeating vows and putting a ring on my finger. Somewhere in between getting engaged and the real-life wedding day arriving I had expected that a house would materialise. And when the shadowy figure in my mind had become a man in army uniform I thought that the house would be one of the little Medway houses used by the army as married quarters in Benbecula. However that was not to be. When we applied for one they were all taken and so we had to join a waiting list and try to rent a local house instead. This was not an easy task at that time in Benbecula, as there were virtually no empty houses around that still boasted a roof, so we decided to try for lodgings for the time being.

My mother somehow settled the matter by arranging for us to share a house with old Benbecula friends of hers, James and Annabel MacPherson, for the few months until a quarter became available or Colin was posted out of Benbecula – whichever happened first. James and Annabel, a brother and sister, were middle-aged and unmarried. They lived in a large bungalow on the borders of Liniclate and Creagorry and they were quite willing to have us share their home. The army was paying a good rent so we were all happy.

Living in Benbecula, so near to Kilpheder, with only a causeway separating us from my parents would seem to be an ideal back-up situation. If I had any problems with my new husband and wanted to back out of the whole marriage thing I could easily go home to mother. But if you think this then you certainly did not know my mother. She had an absolute horror of involvement in her adult children's lives. After they were married that is. Before then she was full of cautions, predictions and advice. Once the ring was on your finger, forget it! It was definitely a case of her enrolment as one of the three wise monkeys. I don't think she would have stood by and watched any of us being hurt or anything like that but as far as complaining to her about husband, wife or married life you just didn't do it as you knew that the shutters would come down. Fortunately nobody in our family tested the water by trying to leave our spouses to move back in with our parents but we have all mentioned the possible outcome over the years and have unanimously agreed that if we had tried it the 'Welcome' mat would not have been in evidence. We were discussing the younger generation's attitude to marriage once and one of my brothers said, 'Go back to Kate MacMillan with a failed marriage? No marriage could be bad enough to make you endure that!' Even in the slightly more enlightened days of the early sixties it would 'cause talk', anathema to my mother and most other Hebrideans of the time.

In the early days of my own marriage life was busy and enjoyable. Any spare time we had together, Colin and I would walk the machair with Skip, our dog, and enjoy the glorious views across the sea to the distant islands. Colin was English but he loved Scotland and the islands in particular. James's bungalow was built on an idyllic spot with a vista of hills on one side and a clear view out to sea on the other. When the wind blew in off the Atlantic in winter it made the lino on the kitchen floor flap about and he would lock the back door and lay a sack filled with sand along the base to stop the draughts. We were near enough to the South Ford, which runs between Benbecula and South Uist, to take a bucket and a couple of rakes and dig for fat cockles when the tide was out, the makings of a tasty supper. Annabel showed us how to put a couple of handfuls of flour in the bucket containing the live cockles and the brine. The cockles ate the flour, didn't like it and spat it out together with any sand or grit which they had ingested that day, so our cooked cockles were entirely free of the nasty grainy bits that set your teeth on edge. I have never in all my travels found cockles to equal the South Ford variety either in size or taste. Between visits and trips with local and army friends, the round of functions in the sergeant's mess and our outdoor activities the weeks flew by.

James and Annabel lived a quiet life and had their own routine built up over many years of peaceful co-existence. Annabel's days were taken up with cleaning, shopping cooking and visiting friends. In the evening she would read or knit whilst listening to Scottish dance music or Gaelic programmes on the radio. James often went to Creagorry Hotel, just down the road, for a drink of an evening but seldom came home the worse for wear. In fact the kitchen floor episode was sufficiently out of character to alarm his sister and excite Skip. I think that James was just unused to being welcomed home by someone who was delighted to see him; even if it was only a dog. All things considered the MacPhersons were very genial hosts and although the situation was not the one I had envisaged when dreaming of married life it could have been a lot worse. We shared the house amicably and Annabel seemed to defer to me in all things to do with housekeeping so that I never felt like an outsider in someone else's home. She was a good bit older than me and spent each tourist season working in hotels in Oban. When autumn came she returned to Benbecula where James had been keeping the home and croft going in her absence and they spent the winter months together.

We had a chat every morning about the 'doings of the day'. If she had something planned as regards laundry or cleaning she'd say, 'I would like to do . . . if that's OK with you, Mrs Hall.' So we never got under each other's feet. She always gave me my full title, which was nice as every new bride gets a bit of a buzz when hearing herself referred to in this way.

Cooking was a combined effort. Colin left early in the morning to get to the range head and so we had breakfast together before the MacPhersons appeared. Lunch for him was a packed box, James took a 'piece' out with him in the morning and seldom came in during the day so Annabel and I would share the table for the midday meal. Dinner was usually a family event, with all four of us sitting down together. Sometimes I cooked (with varying degrees of competence) and at other times Annabel did the honours. She was as nervous as I and always agonized about whether 'Mr Hall' would approve of her efforts. We ate a lot of fresh fish and machair potatoes boiled in their skins, which kept Mr Hall very happy indeed. Annabel had a real fondness for Knorr's asparagus soup, bought in packets, and when it came to deciding the lunch menu she'd say the same thing every day: 'Now about lunch, I was thinking asparagus soup', as if we had never had it before and I would play along and agree that it was a very good idea. As long as it let me out of cooking I'd have eaten boiled seaweed. I always think of Annabel when I see packets of asparagus soup in the supermarket.

The shops at Balivanich were a short walk away and we would go there together most days. Bulk shopping was not really the practice then and, although we bought some items in large quantities, others were bought as and when we were going to use them. Of course we had no fridge or freezer so all perishables had to be bought fresh and used quickly. There were several cousins and friends of Annabel's living in the neighbourhood and I was always included in invitations for a cup of tea and a blether, so although I sometimes missed the busy teaching life which I had given up I was never bored or lonely. Colin worked a long day and after a short time his nasty little major sent him to St Kilda, the isolated outpost leased to the army as an extension to the range, for six weeks, so I had reason to be grateful for Annabel's company.

I also had Skip. One day Colin had come back from the range with a scruffy-looking stray dog that had been running loose on the machair, begging food from the soldiers and generally trying to find a friend. Well, in Colin he found one who not only fed him but adopted him. The MacPhersons were a bit wary at first but once Skip had been cleaned up and a good-looking Border Collie emerged they agreed to let us keep him. That dog was so wise. Although he was still not fully grown he knew exactly which human buttons to press and in no time at all had James and Annabel eating out of his paw. Some days he'd go off with James and at other times he would walk with Annabel and myself to the shops, wearing a collar and lead as if he had been born with them. We never trained him, as he didn't need it. He always just seemed to know what was expected of him and as I've already said, he was always game to join in a midnight sing-song with James.

When we went to Kilpheder to visit my parents my father was delighted with Skip and assured us that the dog looked like a good standard Border Collie. His markings were just right and his intelligence was obvious to anyone. As we had always kept a dog or two on the croft, a succession of working dogs, which became pets and bore names ranging from the usual Scott, Collie, Rex and Sandy to the more fanciful Nancy, Mae (West) and even Tom Dooley, my father knew a lot about dogs. The croft wasn't being worked to the extent that it had been in previous years so the current dog was an old Cairn terrier called Cindy. A boyfriend had given her to me as a present but she had always considered herself to be my father's dog. Although she was very small, even for her breed, she never gave her lack of size a thought and would chase the enormous bemused village bull off our croft if he strayed over from our neighbours' land. When my father went out in the car she would jump on to the passenger seat and go with him. If he had to shop or stop for any other reason she would sleep in the car until he got back and he was always careful to leave the window on her side open so that she had plenty of air. When they returned home and my father parked the car by the gate Cindy would jump out of the window and go into the house. One evening, however, my father was looking for her and couldn't find her anywhere. Then he remembered that she had been with him in the car when he had gone out early in the morning, but he couldn't remember seeing her after that. So he got the car out and took the same route that he had driven earlier and there she was sitting in a lay-by about four miles from home. He had stopped the car there, to let another vehicle overtake him and Cindy, thinking that they were home again, had jumped out. The poor little dog had been sitting there on the same spot all day waiting for her friend to come and find her. She gave Skip a hard time when they first met as he was so much younger than she was and kept wanting to play, but eventually he won her over and they had many a good game together. It was good to go back to the old homestead and I really enjoyed the visits 'up South' to catch up on the local goings on and family news.

I suppose it was a cosy way to be eased into married life. I had all of the status but little of the usual responsibilities. In a way I enjoyed being a 'kept woman' and although ironing thick khaki shirts was new territory at least I never had to clean my husband's boots. Two things my mother-in-law (an ex-army wife herself) had drilled into me were:

Never clean any man's boots and

Never stay behind if he is posted anywhere.

I'm not sure why the boots were taboo, but I knew that Colin's father had abandoned his wife and had left her with a daughter about to be married and two teenaged boys. Presumably the romance with his new wife, a rather mannish ex-WRAC whom I detested on sight, had started whilst he was on an unaccompanied posting. I suppose that if you are away from your wife and family for a long period of time anything in a skirt looks good even if it looks like a Beefeater in drag when you bring it home. Colin's mother was a lovely woman both in looks and personality and to this day I cannot understand how any man could treat her like that. She made a very good job of bringing the family up in days when being a single mum carried no benefits whatsoever. True to her greater wisdom I told Colin that I would not be cleaning his boots, which made him laugh at the very thought, and also that I would be going wherever he went, which didn't seem to bother him at all.

Pretty soon the first posting arrived, before we got our own house in Benbecula. I was a bit sad as I had built a mind picture of that first home in Balivanich married quarters and had been embroidering table mats and buying little bits and pieces for it since my engagement. They were boxed up together with our wedding presents and all the things that we had each accumulated while living our separate lives. One advantage of an army move which I did not appreciate until we started to move house as civilians was the tremendous difference it made to our finances not having to pay for removal costs ourselves. During our army years we lived a very sheltered life in that respect as the Ministry of Defence picked up all costs including storage and all we had to do was pack our stuff, get three estimates from removal companies and they did the rest. On this our initial flitting a lot of our belongings were still in packing cases as the MacPherson house was full of their own furniture, so it was an easy task.

The move was not to a nice sunny destination as we had hoped but to Larkhill Barracks on Salisbury Plain (Colin's fat little major was still riding his broomstick!), however it would be closer to Colin's family and as the artillery regiment that he was being attached to were responsible for the missile tests in the Hebrides we would be going back there from time to time. I was quite happy about it all. The MacPhersons were sad to see us go and tried very hard to persuade us to leave Skip with them, but he was our dog and so wherever we went he would go with us.

My parents were their usual philosophical selves about the move. They knew that they were going to see us again and although they were pleased that we had been fairly near them for some months they covered any signs of grief at our departure by making plans to visit us when we were settled in our new home. All their children had now left the island but with there being six of us there was a steady flow of family coming home for holidays. Although Donald Angus, Donald John, young Donald and Mary Flora all lived in England, Alick, my youngest brother, worked in Glasgow and he hopped on a plane or caught a ferry whenever he had time off, so they weren't alone for any length of time.

We spent the last few days at Kilpheder and we were able to bring my parents a bit of exciting news by telling them that they had a new grandchild on the way. It was not an event which we had planned, but at that time you didn't really plan the arrival of your family, you just left it all to fate and got on with bringing them up. The baby was due just before our first anniversary and although my mother expressed a bit of concern about our nomadic existence we were able to reassure her that we would indeed have a roof over our heads before the event took place. We had just heard that we had again been unlucky with married quarters in Larkhill and would have to split up when we arrived in England. Colin would go in to single accommodation in the barracks during the week and Skip and myself would live with his mother in Bristol until we could rent a house. Colin would join us for weekends and days off. My father was just delighted at the news of the expected arrival of 'Norman'. My two brothers, Donald Angus and Donald John, had a little girl each and they were named Catherine for my auntie and Kay for my mother, now he was sure that his time to be honoured had at last arrived. 'This one is Norman,' he said when we told him and although the baby was probably not much bigger than a decent peanut at the time I knew that it was a boy called Norman, and as usual my father was right.

Before we left we had to have the party; fast becoming

a tradition in the family. If we or any other family member and their spouse had been on the island for a holiday the last night was a write-off. All our friends and relatives would come to wish us well and it would end in a ceilidh to rival the New Year celebrations of yore. A dram or twenty would be had and often the tape recorder, an unwieldy reel-to-reel contraption, would be produced so that we could record our friends' messages and songs to take with us. The idea was that we would be able to have a bit of home with us wherever we were and indeed over the years we spent many an enjoyable evening, on the other side of the world, sometimes in the company of other island exiles, with the Kilpheder ceilidhs for entertainment. Little did we realise when the recordings were being made, that we would still be listening to them long after most of the dear people 'giving their all' were cold in their graves. Some tapes have been transcribed onto modern cassettes and although many have been lost along the way, what we have left can instantly transport us to the living room at 'Brae Lynne', with every chair taken and people sitting on the arms, the tots of whisky, plates of food, the singing and laughing and the clock ticking away towards ferry departure time.

There is nothing quite like the sight of a microphone to bring out the latent exhibitionist in the most unlikely person. Willie Jordan, the Irish packman who had become a naturalised Kilpheder man and a great friend of my father's as well as being a local legend, was no shrinking violet and he loved this opportunity to actually hear himself as he treated us all to a cautionary saga about a nagging wife:

St Peter stood on the Golden Stair
as a man and woman entered there.

The woman was tall and lank and thin
with an edge like a razor on her chin.
The man was quiet and though not stout
he was made with a kind of widening out.
The man stood still, but the woman
she spoke, 'Good St. Peter' said she
'we have come here beseeching thee
to let us into the Heavenly Land
and play the harp in the angel band.
A good life I have led below
sure this man here will tell you so.
I went to church three times a week
and for my neighbours good never feared to speak.
But this, bad man I'm sad to say
He does not walk on the narrow way.
He SMOKES! He DRINKS! Grave faults has he!
He ate all the pantry could afford
while I in penance prayed to the Lord.
But for my sake, Saint Peter, pardon his sins
open the gate and let him come in.'
Saint Peter he leaned on his golden staff
and in spite of his office he had to laugh.
He said to the angel who answered the bell
'Convey this lady down to Hell.'
He turned to the man and quietly said
'How long, my man hast thou been wed?'
The man shook with fear and bowed his head
'Forty years' with a sigh he said.
'FORTY YEARS with a tongue so sharp!
Go, Angel Gabriel, and get him a harp!
Sit him up high where the angels sing
For he deserves to play on the strings,
for the words of the gospel shall come to pass
the last shall be first and the first shall be last!'

I think Willie loved to hear the applause which followed his performance more than anything, as he had spent years entertaining the local population with tall stories and had to endure much ridicule as people got wise to his gift for embroidery. At last he was being appreciated.

Sometimes nerves combined with whisky played tricks with memory and one tape has a little interlude that still makes me smile when I hear it. My father's cousin from Benbecula, Mary Flora MacEachen and her husband Donald John had been great friends of our family from way back. They had come down to wish us farewell on this occasion and as usual the ceilidh was going on and the tape recorder was out, so Donald John volunteered to contribute a duan (poem). He had a slow, nasal way of speaking which comes across very clearly on the recording but unfortunately it was not his greatest moment. I don't know the title or origin of the poem and indeed I can't say that I ever heard it in its entirety as Donald John never got past the first line, *'Dh'fhalbh mi 'nam oinnsich air maduinn Di-Domhnaich'* (I left like an idiot on Sunday morning), pause, *'Dh'fhalbh mi 'nam oinnsich air maduinn Di-Domhnaich'*, pause, *'Dh'fhalbh mi 'n am oinnsich air maduinn Di- Domhnaich'*, pause, and loud and clear in the last of many pauses, his wife's scathing voice in the background, 'Ach for God's sake, give it up!'

Eventually the well-wishers left and we made for our bedrooms to snatch a few hours sleep before being called to the breakfast table by my mother. Although we all went off armed with enough alarm clocks to wake the dead, she herself never went to bed at all on the nights before we left. Ferries seemed to depart at unearthly hours, which meant leaving Kilpheder at the crack of dawn, and as we were never the better for the previous night's carousing we hoped that dawn would crack quietly. My mother, however, did not trust us to heed the alarm bells and would sit with a pile of *People's Friend*, *My Weekly* and other magazines, which my father called 'trealaich' (trash) and read the night away. She kept the peat fires going in the living room grate and kitchen Rayburn, setting the mantel clock to alarm mode 'just in case.'

As we groped our bleary eyed way back into the living room I hope she never realised how difficult it was to eat the full Scottish breakfasts she had fried for us as a last caring act for her departing children. My father, always the more emotional of the two, would be a bit tearful at this stage but would try to crack a joke or two about us having to hurry back so that he could have a decent breakfast again and ask my mother how long she had to practise before frying the perfect plastic egg.

Chapter Two

I CAN'T RECALL MUCH of the journey from Uist to Bristol, but something I will never forget is the sheer terror with which Skip greeted his first tree. South Uist and Benbecula are virtually treeless islands, courtesy of the Ice Age, so the poor dog had never seen a real tree in his life until we stopped the car somewhere on the Oban road to let him do his business. He jumped out, took one look at a grove of trees and howled in terror. One jump got him onto Colin's shoulders and another back into the car and all the time this unearthly wailing howl went on. Eventually we realised what the problem was and we drove away to find a spot of flat treeless ground that was acceptable to him – he performed but still kept looking over his shoulder in case the trees had followed him. It took quite a long time for him to get used to stairs and lifts and traffic during his introduction to mainland life, but it was nothing compared to the time it took to cure him of his tree phobia.

Although I had spent very little time with Nell Hall,

my mother-in-law, prior to the wedding I knew that we would get on well together and the weeks that I spent living with her while Colin commuted to Larkhill Barracks on Salisbury Plain were good fun. She was retired but led a very busy life, seldom in bed after 7.30 a.m. and always on the go. Her flat was in the St Jude's area of Bristol and at that time it was a good place to live. The last time I went there, long after she had left it, the inner city curse of litter, prostitutes and used syringes was much in evidence. In the early sixties you could walk from Nell's flat through a little playing field, cross a bridge over a dual carriageway and find yourself in the middle of the bustling Broadmead shopping area a short walk from the city centre. It was an area convenient for all pursuits such as shopping, sightseeing and travel. As I explored the city, Brunel's feats of engineering and architecture were all around me and history came to life as I walked round the cathedrals, the Cumberland Basin and explored the university library. I was so glad to get to know the place better as I had really liked it when I had visited it, briefly, at the time of my engagement.

Colin's brother lived a bit further out of the city, in Staple Hill, and we spent at least one day a week with him, his wife Beryl and their two young children. Every Tuesday was set aside for a different family gathering. Nell came from a big family of seven girls and two boys. With the exception of one who had married an Australian GI and had emigrated soon after the war, they had all settled in and around Bristol. Every Tuesday since anyone could remember the sisters met and spent the day together taking it in turns to host the weekly gathering, which often included grandchildren and daughters-in-law, at their houses. The husbands wisely found something urgent to do elsewhere on the Tuesday when their house was being used and often appeared as the gathering was breaking up, in time to say 'hello and goodbye'. It was a really amazing way of keeping the extended family in touch with each other and I have not seen it done by any other family before or since. I was roped in as soon as I arrived and before long I had got to know them all.

Each sister had her own 'signature dish' so we always knew what we would be eating for dinner. They were all good cooks and bakers and I was able to collect many recipes to expand my own pitiful fund of culinary knowledge. It soon became evident that the West Country had its own culture, every bit as individual as the Scottish regions, when it came to food and I sampled a lot of their specialities in these early days. There were many things that I never wanted to see or prepare again, let alone eat, after the first introduction. For instance: tripe, chitterlings, brains and elvers – forget it! Tripe and brains were cleaned and boiled then eaten grilled on toast. If you had no hand in the preparation I suppose you could just about stomach them but the cleaning and cooking was a nasty smelly business and so I gave them a wide berth. Chitterlings came cold and cooked, ready to eat from the butcher's and looked like pink curls of luncheon meat. I quite enjoyed them until I was told that they were pig's intestines. Elvers were baby eels, enough said.

The sisters served up the more acceptable steak and kidney pies and puddings, pork steaks and aromatic casseroles, always with their own secret ingredients that they were quite happy to pass on to me but only if I swore not to tell the other sisters. For instance I could not tell anyone that Auntie Ann's Yorkshire puddings were always beautifully light because she put a teaspoonful of vinegar in the batter just before baking them round the roast. When I enthused over Auntie May's Eccles cakes she promptly took me into the kitchen and baked half a dozen there and then so that I could make them exactly like hers, with the secret glaze. It was all done in such a friendly non-patronising way that I felt more like another sister than a raw Teuchter (Islander). My mother-in-law was a good plain cook and her speciality was faggots. Now that was a dish of which I heartily approved and her faggots were the best. Forget the shop-bought variety as they bear little resemblance to Nell Hall's lovely plump spheres of roughly minced pork, liver, onions, bacon and herbs, bound together by fresh breadcrumbs and wrapped in pig's caul. The appetising smell as they cooked could make a hungry man weep. Needless to say whenever it was her Tuesday the sisters demanded faggots, mushy peas and mashed potatoes and they all turned up.

It amazed me how well they all got on and I surmised that their lack of one-up-manship and total honesty with each other had something to do with it. There were no arguments that I recall although they were never afraid to air their views and discuss their differing opinions, mostly on family matters. Goodness knows what they said about me when I wasn't there because if one sister hadn't turned up the guns came out and I learned of her every transgression from birth till that day. As for the absent husbands and children they also got a good going over. While the sisters sat around after the washing up was done they'd all produce knitting or crotchet work from their handbags and tongues and needles would fly. When Norman was born he had the most beautiful collection of matinée coats and pram suits I have ever seen, mostly a product of the aunts and their Tuesday gatherings.

After a few weeks of this semi-detached marriage Colin and I heard that a rented house had become available in Wilton, the village outside Salisbury made famous by its carpets.

It was within easy reach of Larkhill Barracks so we went along for an interview with the owner, a retired lieutenant-colonel. It was a beautiful three-bedroomed detached house on a small estate of five houses just off the Shaftsbury road and as there was a long list of applicants we were delighted when we found that we were successful. It was one of the nicest houses I have ever lived in, all wood blocked floors, Indian carpets and very tasteful furniture and décor. The owner had come back from a long overseas posting and had built it for himself and his wife for their retirement years. He bought her a Mini Cooper so that she could go backwards and forwards to visit her friends and family and all he wanted to do was tend his roses. However, the wife got into the Mini and made for the bright lights never to return, so the poor lieutenant-colonel gave Colin strict instructions about looking after the roses and went off to live with his parents while he arranged a divorce.

My memories of Wilton are pleasant. The people in the other houses were lovely, especially the Freemans who lived across from us. They had a little girl called Christine who had been born with a twisted arm and had undergone many painful operations with little results. She was Skip's best friend as she had an almost identical female version of himself as her pet. As I was fast approaching the end of my pregnancy and feeling like an elephant it was so nice to have Jean and Christine keeping an eye on me, especially as Colin had to dash off to the Hebrides now and then for the missile firings. My original idea of going up with him had to be abandoned as I was in no fit state for arduous travel. It was my first experience of living all alone in a big house, but Skip gave any strange looking person who came to the door the fright of their life so I felt well protected. I took his basket into my bedroom at night and although he snored it was quite a comforting sound.

When Colin was at home we went to some army functions and I got to know some of his colleagues. We had coffee with the neighbours and took some gentle walks through the neighbouring forest of Savernake where Skip finally conquered his fear of trees. There were some lovely pubs in Salisbury and the Star in Wilton became a favourite of ours so we would often end our walk in the vicinity and treat Skip to a packet of crisps while we rested. I was intrigued by the strange place names in the area. One in particular comes to mind, Snail Creep Hanging. Have you ever heard the like?

It is a well-known fact that everyone remembers where he or she was on the evening that President Kennedy was assassinated and I certainly do. I was sitting in the house in Wilton together with my sister-in-law Brenda, who was down from London with my brother, Donald John. It was late evening and Colin had taken Donald John out to the Star for a drink. Their toddler daughter, Kay, was sleeping upstairs and Brenda and I (both in late stages of pregnancy as she was due two weeks after me) were watching Peyton Place on TV when the programme was interrupted by the newsflash reporting the dreadful happenings in Dallas, Texas. We were shocked and tearful as J.F.K. had been such a charismatic man and although much has been said to discredit him since that day most people of our age, especially the women, thought a lot of him. I don't know if it was his film star looks or his aura of leadership but we all thought he was pretty cool. This was the first time that either of us, or many people of the time, had known an assassination – it was a less violent era than that in which we now live – and to witness it being replayed in front of our eyes was blood-chilling.

After a while we turned the TV off and talked quietly, mostly about the awfulness of the situation for Jackie and the children and we both went upstairs to look at little Kay sleeping peacefully through it all. I think it's an automatic human reaction when you hear some catastrophic news to check and reassure yourself that your loved ones are safe. (This was brought home to me just recently when the Twin Towers tragedy occurred and I was here on my own as Colin was out of the country. Every member of my family and many friends from far away to whom I had not spoken for months telephoned me within twenty-four hours.) Having settled down to wait for the men to return we fell silent each of us busy with our own thoughts. Suddenly through the frosted-glass door leading into the hall we saw a shadowy figure moving and heard a ghostly swishing sound followed by a crash. I thought my heart was going to come out of my mouth it was hammering so loudly. Brenda went a greenish white and Skip rushed off and cowered in a far corner of the room well away from the glass door. Well, there were very nearly two accelerated births in that room that night. When we eventually plucked up the courage to investigate we found that someone had made a late delivery of the local paper with some force. It had shot through the letterbox and flown across the hall knocking over a small vase on the telephone table opposite the door. When Colin and Donald John returned from the pub Brenda and I were well in to the brandy.

We had many visits from family and friends during our time at Wilton. Colin's family came and stayed over for weekends, my brothers and sister came down from London and we also had our first visit from Colin's father. Although relations with him had been frosty over the years his sons had kept in touch and, considering the enormous stigma that was attached to divorce when their family had gone through it, I think they did very well by him. He was very comfortably off, with his own business in Southsea and expected, even demanded, frequent contact. I didn't really know what his day with us would be like but apart from my feeling murderous when he took every opportunity to make Colin's accomplishments look like nothing compared to his own army career, the day went well. He was very pleasant to me and complimented me on the nice dinner that I had cooked for him. A few weeks later, on my birthday, I got a present from him, a cookery book. Was I wrong to feel ever so slightly underwhelmed?

The only member of Colin's family whom I yet had to meet was his sister Peggy. She lived in Canada and although Colin and his mother had both been over to see her she had not returned to Bristol since her emigration shortly after the end of the war. Both she and her husband had served their country in the forces but upon demobilising and coming back to the 'Land fit for Heroes' they could find neither work nor a roof to put over their heads. Like so many others at the time they had left the UK with bitter memories. They had prospered in Canada and were very happy there. With four growing children, two of them teenagers, it took much saving up to fund a visit to the old country but at last we heard that they were coming. The visit had been planned as a surprise for Colin's mother and although we were all sworn to keep it a secret from her our excitement was such that it was very difficult to keep quiet about it.

At last the day of their arrival came and Colin and I went to Bristol to be with his mother when they turned up. Colin's brother Ken would meet them at the airport, take them to his house to get freshened up after the long flight and bring them over to Nell's flat, with his own family, in the evening. We had a good day with Nell and all went well until the early evening when she started to get her outdoor things together and we remembered that it was her bingo night, a big problem!

Bingo Night was one of mother-in-law's 'cast in stone' rituals. Once a week she met old workmates from a paint factory called Coulthard and Harding where she had found work in the penniless days after her husband left her. As he had been RSM of the Gloucester regiment she had been 'The First Lady of the Mess' with duties which included hosting cocktail parties and running functions for the wives. She had lived with all the luxury that befitted her husband's rank so working in a paint factory to survive must have been very difficult for her. However she made herself fit in and held down the job for the necessary years. These women had been good friends to her and although times had changed for the better as her alimony etc. came through and she was able to have a modest but debt-free retirement, she never forgot the people who had saved her reason in the bad times. Every week she met up with her factory friends at a Mecca bingo club and once again became one of the girls.

We were in big trouble trying to make her miss her night out and we knew it. Hints about it being a bit rude of her to go out when we were visiting fell on deaf ears and we were afraid that our part of the surprise was about to be ruined. Ken and his wife Beryl had been working behind the scenes for weeks to make sure that there was enough food hidden away, reunions planned, sleeping arrangements worked out etc., and all we had to do was produce Nell at the door when they rang the bell. Now that small task was in jeopardy. We agonised about it all and then Colin had a brainwave; he'd hide her purse. Going to bingo with no money is the equivalent of fishing with no bait, so it worked. She was very upset and I'm afraid that language probably picked up during her factory days was well-aired. She was even more enraged when we refused to lend her any money, pretending to be broke ourselves. So the last, really long, hour before the doorbell rang was spent with a very disgruntled lady.

We were seriously worried about her health as she had a weak heart and she had worked herself up into a lather looking for the purse, and we really hoped that the surprise would not be too much for her. We needn't have worried because when the bell rang all angst was forgotten. When she saw that the face at the door was her daughter's with her husband and children in the background the joy on her own face was a sight to remember forever. The visit went well and was over all too soon.

Little Norman appeared on the scene almost as and when expected but as usual the army tried to interfere. Colin was sent up to Benbecula a week before my due date and although my mother had come out to be with me before and after the birth I really wanted my husband to be around as well. However as it turned out Norman obligingly kept us waiting for ten days and so Colin made it back with a few days to spare. Shortly after he had met his new son he had to go back up to complete the test firings. That period is a bit foggy in my memory.

The reason could have something to do with the fact that I was coping with a new baby but that was a pleasure. Norman was a very easy-going baby with big blue eyes who looked at me as if to say, 'I'm here now, Mum. What do you want me to do?' I had a surge of feeling unlike any other the first time these innocent eyes met mine. It was the strongest feeling I have ever had in my life. After the birth of each of my children I felt a total and unconditional bond with each little person whom I had carried inside me for nine months. I felt a desire to fight the whole world to get a good life for each helpless little scrap of humanity. A mother's love. Unique. The actual birth experience is painful, scary and altogether hellish. There is a lot of total tosh given out about the amazing gains to be had by enduring a natural childbirth. A mystical, ethereal and uplifting experience they call it. 'They' are lying in their teeth. Believe me! Get it over with as quickly and painlessly as possible. Get epidurals, gas anything to ease the pain and once your baby is there, enjoy! When the birth is over you become a different person and you are given a new insight into things which you didn't know before. I understood my father's heartbreak when I was 'given away' to the aunties. I came to understand my mother's wish for me to have a better life even if it meant giving me to someone else to bring up. My outlook on life had completely changed. For the first time ever I had someone who looked at me with an expression which said, 'Hello, I'm new here. Will you look after me? I am helpless without you.' Pretty heavy stuff.

During this time I had to endure the presence of both mother and mother-in-law who had turned up to help and were determined to drive me crazy. They tried to outdo each other in everything, each getting up earlier and earlier in the morning to wash the towelling nappies of the time and start cleaning an already immaculate house. With washing machine and vacuum cleaners booming away at six in the morning I don't think I slept at all during the first two weeks. They were frostily polite to each other and wore my ears off with scarcely veiled grievances and reports of imagined slights whenever the other was out of earshot. I can still see them taking the baby out to a village fête, walking along the Shaftsbury Road, pulling the pram away from each other. My mother put the sun-canopy up and two minutes later Nell had the pram and the canopy was down. It was bad!

Poor Skip didn't know what to make of all this. He hid around the house for most of the day only coming out when his friend Christine Freeman and her little Collie cross 'Lady' came to play with him. He must have felt like a stranger in his own home as he was constantly being told to keep away from the baby's cot by two old women. His mistress always had a baby in her lap and his master was long gone. There was a cot with fluffy things in it where his basket used to be and nobody loved him any more. Eventually, both grannies went home, and Colin came back. When he parked the car and came toward the house carrying his suitcase the dog shot out to greet him, jumped into his arms and urinated all over him.

Chapter Three

A FTER A WHILE OF LIVING in the decidedly superior
Wilton area and having a beautiful house to play
with, it came as something of a shock when the owner
turned up one day to tell us that his divorce was going
through and that he was having to sell the house and give
half of the proceeds to his estranged wife. He thanked us
sincerely for keeping it and the roses in such good order
and very generously offered to let us have first refusal on
the property at a special price of £5,000. This was the
early sixties so it was a good price, especially as he was
willing to leave all the furniture apart from some small
portable personal items. We were very tempted and tried
to work out how we could do it.

If we bought the place we could always rent it out
when we had to leave the area and it would be a great
investment. We could get a mortgage without any
problem, but although we had some money saved we
were £500 short of the deposit required of us as first time
buyers. The bank was out of the question as we did not

think it would be a good idea to have a bank loan and a mortgage to pay off at the same time on army pay, so we decided to ask Colin's father for an interest-free loan of £500 which we could manage to pay off fairly quickly without the charges which a bank would add. Although his business was doing well and he always gave the impression that he was very affluent indeed Colin's father turned us down; he said we were a bad risk. Over the years neither Colin nor myself I have ever shirked work, welshed on a debt or been short of money and we have bought and sold houses at more than twenty times the price of that one. We have often spent £500 on some frivolous whim or gift for the children without even thinking about it, so he'd have got his little bit of money back and we could have had a good start and a fine house as security, but father-in-law did what he had always done for his children, try to make them feel small. It might have had a good effect on them as they have all succeeded in their lives, who knows?

Fortunately a married quarter became available just at that time and not wishing to hang about showing prospective buyers round the house we decided to cut our losses and move. So we moved into a first-floor flat in Larkhill Barracks, with worn lino on the floor. It was painted a dull grey throughout with a diagonal crack in the living room wall stretching from the skirting board on one side to the ceiling on the other. If we waited for the army decorators to come and redo the place we could be waiting for months so we got going with paint and paper, scattered our wedding presents around, bought a few rugs and soon transformed the place. We already knew a few of our neighbours and were soon feeling quite at home. Skip, however, was not at all happy with our new home. He was quite a big dog and a flat was not really the place for him. Apart from a few weeks of flat dwelling when we were living with Colin's mother there had always been a back door he could run through and a garden he could play in; now he had none of the liberty which he had become used to. Once Norman started crawling and trying to walk the dog had a worrying tendency of shepherding him into a corner and baring his teeth, so I could never leave them alone in the same room. With great sorrow we decided that our dear but confused dog had to go. Colin advertised in *The Farmer's Weekly* and a sheep farmer answered the advert. So Skip went off to do what he was meant to do, herd sheep on a hill farm. Colin went over once or twice to check on him and although he arrived unannounced the dog was obviously happy and well looked after. He had been promoted to lead dog the last time Colin saw him and the sheep farmer tried to give us £50 for him as he said that he had never had such a good dog. Colin said that it would be like selling a child and refused the money asking only that Skip continue to be well cared for. The dog didn't make any fuss of his previous master and when he was leaving just ran off to do his job. We missed him sorely and then and there we decided not to have any more dogs until we could give them the security of a permanent home. Brave words.

Larkhill was a bit of a faceless place. It was a soldiers' town and dominated by uniforms. There were many activities for the families and an abundance of babysitters were available so we had a good social life. There was a large artillery regiment based there as part of the School of Artillery plus support groups from other regiments, including Colin's REME workshops, so the mess life was fantastic. I had to buy my first of many full-length evening gowns, as most of the functions required you to wear formal dress. Boy, it was a lovely dress! Black velvet, straight skirt with slit. Black satin band under the bust, deep V neck front and back. Black satin shoulder straps. My first evening dress and the best. It cost £15 and I know that I looked fantastic! The poor men only had to change into mess dress which made them all look very dashing but involved no shopping so we women had the best of the bargain there. The mess was always beautifully decorated with floral arrangements, glittering chandeliers and regimental silver twinkling away. The bands provided excellent music and the buffets covering tables which stretched the whole length of the building were perfection in artistic presentation and taste. Think of the best cruise ship buffet you have ever seen and it doesn't even come close. Yes indeed, being an army wife in peacetime had much to recommend it. I had to learn to do a bit of bowing and scraping to the wives of higher-ranking officers but I stuck my tongue firmly in my cheek and got on with it.

We were close to Salisbury, a cathedral town with an almost mediaeval feel about it especially if you walked around it on Wednesdays or Saturdays when the farmers came to town for the street market. Amesbury was another little country town close by. If we wanted something a bit special we went to Birmingham and invaded the Bullring shops. I had not been at Larkhill for very long before I was roped in to do some supply teaching at the local school and as they had a crèche for Norman it was rather nice to get back to my job again. Norman was a very portable baby and revelled in the attention of the carers. Before too long, just as we were beginning to settle, another posting came through, a sunny one at last, Malaysia and Singapore. First however, Colin had to go back to Benbecula for some months and as there was a house available for us we went as a family. I was a bit sad leaving the grotty flat, which we had made into a comfy home, but my sadness turned to anger when we were 'marched out'. Marching out was the name given to the inspection which took place before army personnel vacate a quarter. The 'Marching Out' squad scrutinised everything and made you quake in your shoes in case they found any dirt or breakages. I just couldn't believe my eyes when they wrote, 'Living room walls papered without authorisation. Departing soldier will be charged for having walls stripped and painted if incoming soldier requires it.' Well they couldn't charge us for the crack that we had filled in. Whoever moved in must have been quite happy with our efforts as we heard no more about it.

So it was back to the islands again and a very strange feeling it was, going back as an army wife. At first we had to live in Kilpheder with my parents for a few weeks until our quarter was ready and I must say that that experience did not live up to my expectations. I did not feel too comfortable sharing the house with my parents and although Norman was a very easy baby I was always being told that I was spoiling him, ignoring him, giving him too much, too little to eat etc., and as child number two was already on the way I wondered if I would ever be a good enough mother to see either of them into their schooldays alive.

The weekends were lovely as Colin was off and we could go down to Kilpheder machair and let Norman crawl around in the sand and eat seaweed. In fact he took his first stumbling steps trying to get into the wavelets at the edge of the sea. During the week Colin was in Benbecula or on the range in Gerinish all day so I often

put Norman in the pushchair and walked out to
Leonard Place, the little group of houses on the
Kilpheder–Lochboisdale road where my retired teacher
aunt and her sister, my foster parents of childhood days
lived. They had never seen eye to eye with my father and
throughout the days when I had lived with them as a
child in Benbecula and Barra I had to endure many
homilies about his shortcomings. As they all grew older
the bickering went on and I found it very difficult
listening to Auntie Chirsty, the older of the two asking,
'*Ciamar a tha an ceard ruadh a ghoid mo chruit?*' (How
is the red haired tinker who stole my croft?). According
to the custom of the time my grandfather had bequeathed
his croft to my father, as he had no surviving sons and the
aunties, although older than my mother, were unmarried.
Incidentally, my father came from a very respectable
family who wouldn't have a clue how to make a pail or a
clothes peg so the tinker jibe was a figment of a bitter
imagination. Anyway I kept my counsel most of the time
but one day it got too much and I put Norman back in
the pushchair and practically ran the two miles home.
That little marathon nearly lost me my second child and I
had to have a few days flat on my back before I could do
anything again. On reflection, now that I know how
pregnancy heightens your sensitivities, I think that I may
have been overreacting all round.

My old friends of single days, Jean and Dorothy, had
left the island but another dear friend from my childhood
days in Barra had married a Kilpheder man and they had
built a house just down the road from us. Her name was
Chrissie MacIntyre and although, tragically, she died a
few years later I will never forget her. She had got to
know my father and mother well whilst I was away in
England and was a lifeline to sanity for me during the

weeks when my mother and I were fighting for control of the kitchen. Beautiful Chrissie, with her blue-black hair, clear grey eyes and the only true peaches and cream complexion I have ever seen, would give one of her gurgling laughs and say, '*Cha toill da chearc ann an aon nead, fuirich gus an teid thu a' Bhala Mhanaich 's bi sibh cho reith ri reith. Feuch nach marbh sibh a cheile neo cha bhi tigh ceilidh agamsa 'nuar a dh'fhalbhas tu.*' (Two hens can't share the same nest. You wait until you've moved to Balivanich and you'll both be friends again. Don't kill each other or I won't have a house to visit when you've left!)

Chrissie was right. As soon as we got our married quarter things changed completely and friendly relations were quickly restored. We had some happy times there and a lot of visits from the parents. If I learnt anything at all during that time it was that once you have had control of your own home and family you can never go back to living in your parent's home and pick up where you left off. A lot of the tension during our stay in Kilpheder was caused not, as I thought, by our presence but by the continuing bouts of drinking which my father had engaged in during our absence. Money was not very plentiful and although this never really caused any trouble between my parents, the aunties would make a big issue of it. They were always giving my mother money accompanied by a lecture on her husband's profligate behaviour. My father was well aware of this and resented it, but could not do anything about it. He maintained that he had worked hard all his life and was entitled to the occasional spree. A common Hebridean philosophy and not a bad one if kept under control. However the aunties did not see it this way. He had to pass their house whenever he had to go to Lochboisdale and they were always watching the road. He was going to the hotel, by their way of thinking, so the next time my mother would visit them she'd get a lecture. It was bound to cause friction as I had found out for myself.

On Sundays the aunties went to mass at St Peter's church, down the road from our house and would come to Brae Lynne for their dinner with my parents. One Sunday, shortly after Colin and I had moved to our married quarter, my mother was feeling a bit off colour and didn't go to church but when my father came back with the aunties she had dinner ready for them as usual. They had hardly sat down when they started in on the questions. 'Where was Norman going last Tuesday at half past two? We saw the car going out to Lochboisdale. He was going drinking wasn't he?' And so it went on. Any time my father left the room the vitriol would pour again and when he returned they would change the subject and pretend to be talking about someone else. Eventually my mother, who was not feeling well, had had enough and she told them to mind their own business and start behaving like Christians as they had just been to church. Oh dear, this was the last straw for Auntie Chirsty and she got up and started putting her coat on saying 'Come on, Catherine, we are not going to eat off the same table as people who speak to us like that after all you've done for the family.' My mother was walking through from the kitchen with a plate of roast lamb, potatoes, vegetables and gravy in each hand and when she heard this something snapped. She shouted, 'You won't eat off our table, then eat it off the wall!' and she threw the plates at the opposite wall. My mother was always a placid peace-loving person but when she lost it it was always spectacular. The aunties beat a very hasty retreat along the Kilpheder road and my parents washed the wall down, had their dinner in peace and laughed for a week. When they told us about this we laughed too, but I could understand the strain they lived under.

In the old days our car was an old Morris Traveller PUS 85, a kind of family car which had been well used by all of us. After we had all left home my father sold it and bought a new dark-green Ford Zephyr. It was a lovely car and despite the fact that as it was the only one of its kind on the island it was instantly recognisable by the aunties, it was my father's pride and joy. One evening he and my mother came to visit us and the car had a huge dent right in the middle of the rear nearside door. We couldn't figure out what had happened as the dent was full of scratches and although very deep it did not have the smaller fading-out kind of indentations that your car shows when it has collided with another vehicle. Then we heard the tale. He had taken a neighbour out to the moor to look for lost sheep and had parked the car by the side of the road. On their way back they could hear this almighty racket and there was a big ram beating the living daylights out of his own reflection in the car door. I don't know what the insurance company thought when they read his claim but he swore that he would never polish the car again. They were good the visits, always a tale to tell and always a laugh or two, although a certain sadness was creeping into my mind. These two people, and my father in particular, had been my icons all my life and now I was about to go to the other side of the world for three years. What would that time hold for them? I wished that I could stay and make it all come right for them. I could feel their sadness, their sense of loss as all their children had left home and nobody wanted to know about the croft any more ... except Aunty Chirsty. For them the world had changed but not for the better. Their children had been encouraged to leave the islands and find a better world, now they were alone. Is there a better life? I've seen most of it and I don't think so.

Philip came shouting into the world early one October morning in Daliburgh hospital. A completely different baby to Norman, but equally adorable. Weighing in at 10lb 14oz he was big, hungry, frowning and had huge navy-blue eyes totally crossed. He had black hair hanging to his shoulders and all the nurses loved him and called him 'Ringo' after the Beatle. Once again I was completely enraptured and the thought that I had nearly lost him made him doubly precious. Apart from the aforementioned awful aspects of childbirth – yes it always hurts – I thoroughly enjoyed my stay in hospital. The nurses, Joan MacKinnon, Rona MacDonald (Lightfoot) and Katie MacLellan (MacMillan), were all well known to me from way back. Joan was the mother of a school friend, Catriona and Rona and Katie had been at school with me. We had some talking to do, I can tell you. I shared a room with Martha MacKinnon (MacEachen), an old friend from Convent Days in Fort William and as the Irish would say 'the craic was great!' There were still some Sacred Heart nuns running the hospital and once or twice one of them came in and asked us to keep the laughter down . . . shades of the old days. The care of mothers and babies was exceptional and I really appreciated it, especially after enduring the questionable attention of two very mannish Queen Alexandra nurses in the military hospital in Tidworth when Norman was born. Philip was even better looking when his big blue eyes straightened out and by the time I took him home to meet his eighteen-month-old brother, with all the extra bottle feeds Joan had smuggled in to him during the night, he had stopped shouting. Norman said 'Hello, baby' and hit him with a hairbrush.

Ah me, the days of being the only grandson had finished for poor Norman, and I had to keep a sharp eye on him when he pottered around the house, especially if he had anything in his hand which could be used as a weapon. His grandfather adored him and took him out to see the cows and generally kept him out of harm's way as much as possible until he got used to the new baby.

At this time things became somewhat unstuck for me. In retrospect I think my orderly life had become a bit chaotic and I was packing again ready for the Far East posting. To make matters even more difficult Colin had to go to Pembroke to do a couple of months' training in Manorbier immediately before embarkation. It meant packing all our stuff and going to the other end of the country, before coming back again to London to join a new regiment and fly to Singapore. I have no recollection of feeling bad or anything but I must have alarmed Colin because before I knew what was happening Norman was left with Mum and Dad, Philip was being looked after in London by my sister-in-law, Sheila, and I was on holiday in Paris with Colin! It was bitterly cold and I enjoyed the Louvre and Sacre Coeur, bought a beautiful red suit in Galleries Lafayette and generally regained my sense of humour. We took a train to Germany and spent some time with our friends from Larkhill, who were now attached to a regiment that was serving in Osnabruk. Then the two weeks were up and we collected our babies and headed for home. Sheila had loved looking after Philip and she immediately became pregnant and had a little boy herself, Gordon, a brother for Catherine.

When we got back to Benbecula it was all systems go, packing, and generally getting ready to move out. Then it was another farewell party at Brae Lynne and off we went. My father was very sad to see us go as he and Colin got on really well and he knew that the children would grow up without any recollection of their granddad. It didn't really bother me all that much as I knew that we would be back in three years. Sadly now that I am older myself I can understand his feelings so much better. When you get to a certain age the future is no longer a certainty. My mother was made of sterner stuff and she and the aunties, who were speaking to us again, said their goodbyes to us with smiling faces.

We were a really raggle taggle company, with all our personal luggage and the kit you need for two children under two heaved around from Lochboisdale to Bristol and then on to Pembroke where a friend from Colin's bachelor days met us and took us to our lodgings. As we were only going to spend two months there we didn't stand any chance of getting a married quarter but had managed to get a flat at the top of a very posh old house right on the sea front. It sounds delightful but it was nothing of the sort. It was filthy and the rooms were very large. To be honest I don't think that I ever finished cleaning it. I merely made part of it habitable and left the rest for the next summer visitors to sort out. We used one bedroom, with a double bed, a single bed and a cot and the first night we were so cold that we all ended up sleeping in the same bed! The heating was minimal and fed by a meter with a voracious appetite so we learned to keep a pile of ten pence pieces right next to it and put a few in every time we passed it.

We were not allowed to use the front entrance to the house as its owner, a real old skinflint of a lady lived on the ground floor. Instead we had to use a fire escape that came down the side of the house when we entered and left. This was not too bad if we were going somewhere as a family, but picture the scene during the day if I had to hang washing out, or fill the coal scuttle. Norman was still a bit too unpredictable to be left in the same room as Philip, so I had to get myself well padded to resist the biting wind, pad Norman up, and then descend the fire escape with Norman under one arm and the washing basket or coal scuttle in the other. One thing Norman learned very quickly was to hold on tight as I really needed three arms to get to the ground with any guarantee of safety.

Mick Bailey, Colin's friend who had met us, and his wife, Pat, were frequent visitors and although he had laughed himself silly when he saw his bachelor friend Colin get off the train with a wife two babies and a mountain of luggage, he proved to be a good friend to us. They lived in married quarters with their young son and I often spent the afternoon with Pat either at her house or at ours. The little boy, whose name escapes me, was a little bit older than Norman and he had a huge playpen full of little cars which he had lined up in perfect order. Norman would get into the playpen with him and start making another line of cars at the other end of the playpen and so they would spend the afternoon in perfect harmony, chuntering away to their cars while Philip slept and their two mothers put the world to rights.

Chapter Four

I WILL NOT EVEN TRY TO describe the last few days before leaving for the Far East . . . the bedlam of packing, getting ourselves to Bristol to say goodbye, then on to London to see my brothers and sister and finally getting everything ready to take to the airport in good time to find that all the London taxis had decided to go on strike that morning! Well, my family were magnificent: brothers, sister, in-laws, all of them carrying suitcases swarmed onto underground and trains and got us to the airport with not a second to spare. The rest of the regiment was assembled in the waiting room and after we said a very quick goodbye to all our family, we were rushed onto the plane without making any contact at all with our new company. They trooped on after us and a very unfriendly lot of people they seemed to be . . . With all the fuss that had been made of us they all thought that Colin was the new Colonel and nobody spoke to us all the way to Kuala Lumpur airport.

Travel was not such an everyday occurrence then and I

think we were very fortunate to have a really nice aeroplane to fly in and the usual kind of service that we have now come to expect and is so essential when you are travelling with two babies, so the actual flight was a bit of a blur. However, nothing that has happened since in my life has obliterated the feeling of my first landing in Kuala Lumpur. If I close my eyes now so many years later, I can still smell it. It had been raining in the evening and we landed fairly late, the smell of the freshly washed flowers, the pitch-black sky, the bright stars, it was magic. It doesn't matter what you see afterwards the first sight of something really astounding stays with you, and to me my first sight of the Far East was the stuff that dreams are made of. It didn't matter that my husband and I had two children under two, no friends at all in this new company, not a clue about our futures, my first taste of the Far East was enough to make me feel that nothing that would ever happen to me could take away this moment. And it hasn't.

The mistake about our status had been rectified pretty soon after landing when other members of Colin's corps started to recognise him and came to introduce their wives and kiddies and soon we all joined up and became a group. A pretty strange group really. There was a Welsh girl, some English girls, a German girl and yours truly who was proudly Hebridean, but we all had one thing in common, little children and the excitement of not having a clue where we were going or what our new homes would be like.

We were bussed to the garrison in Tampin where we had to assemble in the sergeants mess and be sorted out. The children by this time were all a bit tired and fractious and I was so glad that mine were young enough to respond to the cuddle, bottle, sleep routine as by now our journey had taken the best part of a week from the rather slapdash but stable home in Manorbier. The beauty of the countryside still had me in its grip and although we had journeyed through some incredibly poor areas where natives lived the general wild splendour of the flowers and shrubs still enthralled me. I wasn't at all surprised to find that our new home, when we finally had it allocated, was a lovely bungalow in about a quarter of an acre of immaculate garden with a banana tree in full fruit nodding in one corner. Two servants greeted us, an old Chinese lady and her granddaughter, Soom and Kio, and with much bowing and scraping and many smiles made us a cup of tea. The house was immaculate and I just knew that I would be happy there.

Unfortunately the first night was a bit of a shock. First of all we were in the last married quarter in the group, right on the edge of the jungle and when the daylight faded, quite early in the evening, and the servants had gone home, all hell broke loose. The noise of the jungle nightlife was indescribable. The calling and hooting of gibbons, the wailing and caterwauling of some unknown creatures, and the occasional bump on the roof of the house were minor difficulties; our main problem was the almighty racket which came from the loft. Bats! There was not too much rest had in that house until Colin had got rid of them in a manner that is best left to the imagination. It took a few nights before we got any sleep worth talking about. We gradually got used to the outside noises and got on with our lives.

The army married quarters were all fairly close together and although they were all built in the same way, bungalows with a reasonably sized plot, the fact that local labour was cheap meant that the wives could really go to town on the flowers and bushes and every garden was a picture. Of course we did no gardening ourselves: the locals were not very wealthy and any job, from cleaning your shoes to having a complete new wardrobe beautifully sewn, was yours for a very reasonable sum. Most of the women were very happy to slot into this way of life and spent most of their time having coffee mornings, going to the swimming pools and generally living the life of Riley but the men were not so lucky. Ten days after we landed, a troop of them were sent to Borneo for three months, to stop the Indonesians from invading Borneo. Naturally Colin was one of them. Just before he left the Headmaster of the Camp school had been to see me and had offered me a job so that was that.

The rest of our time in Malaysia took on a slightly different pattern to that of the other army couples. I was teaching from eight thirty till one o'clock, that was the general knocking off time for all schools as it got far too hot in the afternoon for the children to be in any way fit to concentrate. My own children were quite happy to be slaved over by Kio and apart from a slight altercation when she trimmed Norman's eyelashes in the Chinese style her care of them was excellent. In the afternoons I took them swimming and Norman was well happy and could keep himself afloat with a rubber ring right from the start. Philip was growing into a lovely smiling toddler and spent most of his afternoons being amused by the attentions of the other children and of course his proud mum. I was always a bit afraid of the water, a throwback to my childhood in the Hebrides, where the currents were so unpredictable that you had to be a very strong swimmer to survive. We were never encouraged to try to learn how to swim so I was always a bit wary of the swimming pool. I did join a swimming club along with my friends in the hope of learning but I nearly drowned the instructor so I gave that up.

While the men were away we had plenty of opportunity to enjoy our evenings, as there was a troupe of soldiers who were in charge of entertainment and organised everything from concerts to bingo and sent transport round to pick up the wives who couldn't drive. There was always a marvellous buffet laid on and as you sat with your friends in your latest evening dress it was easy to forget the purpose of your existence in that peacetime army. We, the wives, were treated so well, as long as we behaved ourselves. There were one or two who could not bear the absence of their men and had short-lived affairs but they were very quickly sent back to England in disgrace while the rest of us tut-tutted and got on with life.

I have always had an almost pathological fear of snakes and sure enough the night after Colin left for Borneo I found a bootlace snake under a chair. As it wriggled and reared at me I grabbed an empty milk bottle and I was screaming and bashing away at it for minutes after the poor thing was dead. I saw quite a few snakes after that and never got over my hatred of them, big or small . . . yuk! I made sure that the dustbin was always tied to the branches of a tall tree in the garden and always turned my shoes over and gave them a tap before putting them on in case any small snake had made a bed in there during the night. There were a few other beasties, which we had to be wary of, mainly creatures with which we were familiar in the UK but were three times the size and more venomous in Malaysia. Poor Norman came to understand that when he picked up a very poisonous six-inch long beast of a centipede. It was huge and with its many legs it looked lethal enough to frighten me, but the children were not at all frightened of the wildlife. However, this centipede promptly bit and filled Norman's little wrist with venom. He screamed and dropped it. When I saw what had attacked him I put it in a jar and took him to the doctor. His wrist was swelling and by the time we got to the surgery the swelling was advancing half way up his arm in an angry red bulbous line.

The doctor was not very helpful at first refusing to believe that a centipede could do such damage until I produced the jar and showed him the culprit. He was pretty shocked then and promptly gave Norman some anti-venom injections. The poor little boy was already feeling drowsy and took a few days to get over the attack. The doctor took the centipede and had it up on his wall with a poster warning people not to handle the wildlife unless they were sure of the creature's potential danger. After that Norman had a much more sensible attitude to creepy crawlies and called them 'Killits'.

Teaching in Tampin School was very nice. The children in my class were well behaved and our staff was a good bunch of young British teachers who had officer status and lived in the officer's mess. The headmaster and his wife had a nice house in the officer's quarters and as I was a member of staff I had honorary officer status and could use the officer's mess if I wished. However I never did as I was more than happy with what the sergeant's mess had to offer in the way of entertainment and from what I heard the officer's mess was dead boring anyway. The rebel in me came out occasionally and I narrowly missed trouble once or twice. Once, when I was picked up by one of the teachers in her sports car who'd had a heavy night the night before (well she was single and young and who could blame her) so I was driving. When we came to the gate going into the camp it was closed and there was no sentry on duty so I drove under the gate and on to the school. This became our standard way of entry until one day when we drove to school together she tried the same trick and we heard the click of a gun being cocked and a furious voice shouting 'Halt!' which we did very smartly. The guard had been alerted to our habit and was told to shoot our tyres if we ignored him. Another trick I learned was that I could get to the post office to pick up my mail very quickly at play time if I took a short-cut through the Strictly Private part of the camp and ran past some offices. I was doing this one day when I heard the colonel's voice coming out of one shouting, 'There's that damned woman again, if she runs past my office one more time shoot her!' I don't know if he meant it but I never took the risk of finding out.

It was a busy time for me but I was very happy. The children were well and did not seem to pick up the ailments that some of the other kids suffered from. When the monsoon season started in earnest and we had pouring rain for a few hours every afternoon most of the other children came out in blisters. They were big round water blisters and we called them 'Monsoon Blisters'. If you didn't burst them they went away after a few days but burst one and the fluid which it contained started off another crop. I believe that they were also very itchy and so we had a very blistery younger generation for a while. Fortunately neither of the boys were affected.

Soon Colin was back and we were planning a trip to the Army Holiday Centre in Penang. We had to wait until his leave coincided with my school holidays and away we went. It was quite memorable and this was not only because of the splendour of the scenery and the excellent entertainment. One day we were swimming and sunbathing on the beach when we noticed that Norman, who was in the water with his rubber ring, was drifting a bit too far out to sea and did not respond to our calls telling him to come back, so Colin went off to fetch him. Well, the reason he was drifting became apparent to Colin as soon as he got to him and found that there was a strong undertow in that spot and it took him all his time to turn around and swim back to shore towing Norman who thought it was all brilliant fun. I shudder to think what could have happened had we not been so vigilant. Another night we hired a babysitter and went out to a dance. When we came back Colin took the babysitter home and I was getting ready for bed when I noticed a snake hanging from the rails which held up the mosquito nets around our bed. It was a fairly large snake and it writhed around this way and that as I shot out of the door on to the entranceway screaming, 'Snake! Snake!' Fortunately I bumped into Colin who had returned and he went in and put the lights on. My snake was his tie, which he had taken off and slung over the net rails before taking the babysitter home. There was a fan above it causing it to move in a very snake-like fashion. Umm! Enough said. It was a good job that the babysitter lived on the camp or I'd have had an even redder face to go with my undies.

Shopping in Tampin was a joy with all the jewellery and beautiful carvings. Fortunately my convent days had left me with a tendency to 'window shop' rather than be coerced into actually parting with too much money. I did, however, buy some ornaments and had a camphor-wood chest made which is still admired by all who see it. It is made from teak in two colours and lined with camphor wood that gives a lovely smell to any linen stored in it. The outside is very nicely carved and it has a beautiful brass lock. We also treated ourselves to some small tables and a lamp in carved Malacca wood. (We shouldn't have bothered with those as the wood had not been properly seasoned and they fell apart when we brought them back to England.)

It was difficult for me to get used to the chasm that had appeared between myself and my family in the UK at first. There was a lack of phone calls as it was well nigh impossible to get through and the mail came in bundles so there was a long time with nothing then three or four letters from the same person. However, like everything else we got used to it and thankfully there were no deaths or bad illnesses to report from either side during that period. Soon we were told that the next eighteen months were to be spent in Singapore and we all packed up and got ready to leave lovely Tampin. At least we were all going together and although none of my particular group of friends had been to Singapore before we didn't think it could be all that much different to Malaysia.

Singapore was a different place altogether. It lacked the charm of Tampin as it had such a large multi-ethnic community. The inhabitants were mostly Chinese but with many other people of various colours and creeds making a good living there. Selerang barrack buildings were old and imposing and we actually had our married quarters in part of what had once been Changi jail. Our house used to hold as many prisoners as could be stood up together, during the war. Now there's a thought. It was a beautiful building, a terrace of houses as far as the eyes could see, on a hill about a mile from Changi. Across the road was a valley, which we called Snake Valley, and nobody crossed that particular piece of ground even in broad daylight, as we all had a healthy fear of snakes. A road went round the valley and into one of the most impressive army camps I have ever seen. The buildings were palatial and to see a ceremonial occasion there was something really special. A company of Lifeguards shared the camp with us and their ceremonies (to which we were always invited) were quite spectacular. I had a Lifeguard family living on either side of me and although they were both fresh from Buckingham Palace I could not wish for nicer neighbours. Boy, they had some tales to tell!

Our amah (maid) was Chinese and her name was Lim Tu. She was wonderful. She and Philip instantly fell in love and she did all my housework with him either on her back or tucked under her arm. All the maids used to wear flip-flops, all the same kind in various bright colours and they left them outside the door of the house in which they worked. Philip would wander along the back veranda and collect them all when the spirit moved him. He would then put them back but never in the right order so at the end of many a day I would hear the cry of 'Oh Philip!' and much laughter as the amahs tried to sort out whose shoes were whose. Norman was old enough to go to the Camp nursery school and it was Philip's ambition to join also, so anytime he went missing we only had to go up to the nursery school and there he'd be sat on the teacher's lap. In the end they ignored the fact that he was a good six months too young and let him go with his brother whenever he fancied a day at school.

Shortly after we got to Singapore Colin got his Long Service and Good Conduct medal and although I would have liked to be there to see him decorated it was a men only occasion. However the photo looked good and after twenty years of service Colin didn't look bad either. He also got a medal for his service in Borneo to add to the one he had received before I met him, when he had been

51

shot at during a previous stint in Malaysia when Communist terrorists had tried, unsuccessfully, to take over the country.

I did a little bit of supply teaching at the Camp school but truth to tell I was a bit tired of work and wanted to go to the crocodile farms and shopping in Change Alley and see a bit more of the country with my friends. I was also getting a taste for whist and enjoyed the morning drives which we organised at each other's houses (very popular with the Lifeguard wives). And so the eighteen months in Singapore were more like eighteen months of wonderful holiday time for me. Colin had to go to work and go off on exercise periodically. He also played golf and of course there were many evenings when we both got dressed to kill and went to the mess to some function or other. My first evening dress bought while I was at Larkhill now had several companions and getting a new one run up by the dressmaker was never a problem.

Norman and Philip had made friends with some of the other 'tinies' and after nursery school they would all congregate with their tricycles and play happily while the ever vigilant amahs chattered away and watched that they came to no harm. There was a wide pavement-type path that went down the front of the houses and as the children used it as a playground it was really easy to spot anyone who was in trouble. One day, however, Philip got loose and went wandering down the back of the houses. He found a piece of an old bath which a workman had left in the monsoon drain and picked it up. It was about two inches by three and had become razor sharp around the edges with being left outside in the monsoon rain. He trotted along with this clenched firmly in his fist. The amah had missed him and was soon on his track so he began to chuckle and run to evade her. He was looking over his shoulder and laughing when he tripped and fell. She picked him up and cuddled him noticing that he'd gone very pale and didn't seem to be breathing. In fact he was holding his breath and when he let out an almighty shout of pain she started to look for grazes on his knees and was shocked to see the blood pouring out of his little hand. He had fallen on to the hand which held the piece of sharp porcelain. She ran back to the house with him and we found that the middle finger of his right hand was slashed right through to the nail, all the way round the top. In fact the skin had detached itself and was like a hood over the nail. It makes me feel sick thinking about it. Colin immediately got the car out and we took Phil to the doctor. The most amazing thing to me is that he only cried for the first few minutes, even the doctor was full of admiration for him and said as he stitched his finger, 'You are a wee soldier, sonny!' Well, Philip still has the scar on his finger but can't remember it hurting. He talked non-stop all the way to the doctor and back, mostly 'scribble talk' but as we passed the airfield at Changi he lifted his bandaged hand and said his first clear word, 'helicopters'. From that moment all his speech seemed to come in bursts and in a few weeks he could talk for Africa.

We had some great parties in Singapore. As the houses were all in a line it was so easy to have everybody to your house, have the amah bake and cook delicious Chinese titbits for you and lay them out. Lim always stayed the night when we had a party as it was easier for her than getting up early in the morning to catch the bus to get to us and often she would sit outside her quarters talking to our guests and giving them advice on cooking and ailments. Her mother always sent us a package of special, very large, prawns all cooked and ready to be put on the table. No money would be accepted, and she always included a prawn specially decorated for Philip and a tiny crab with tissue paper clothes for Norman. Lim had the boys home with her one day and brought photos in of them swimming with herself and her boyfriend and generally having a good time. There seemed to be a certain rivalry between the amahs about which one was best thought of by their employers. Well, Lim was wonderful, young and quiet but always immaculately dressed and she kept the house and us all in very good order.

Colin was a keen card player when he was away from home and I still have a beautiful gold bracelet brought for me from Borneo for which he'd paid all his illicit earnings! However one morning he came home from a spell away and confessed that the car had to go. He had lost a considerable amount and had bargained with his opponent who agreed to accept the car in payment. It was a dreadful old car and I never drove it anyway, but it cured Colin of his gambling, so that was something to be supremely thankful for! There was really not much need for a car in Singapore as you just had to go on to the main road and wait for a few minutes and a taxi would come hurtling along. It didn't matter how many people were in there already they would cram you in and charge you a very modest fare to get you to your destination. The taxis were all Mercedes and kept very clean, and you didn't mind if you were the only white person in there you never felt in any way threatened.

We were delighted to find that two people who had been at Daliburgh school with me, Rhoda and Donald Walker, were in Singapore at the same time as us, although at a different garrison, and we saw quite a lot of them and their little son. They were the only islanders I saw for three years but it was great to get together from time to time and catch up on the bits of island news which we'd had from our irregular post. The islands and their inhabitants had become a bit far away in the exalted life that we now lived and it was great to get together with Rhoda and have a good natter in Gaelic from time to time. We had both been regular singers at the concerts at home before our marriage and Donald had sat behind me in Daliburgh School for three years so it was always a very jolly occasion when we visited each other. Colin and Donald got on very well together and their little boy and our two played very well, being of similar ages.

Of course the women from Tampin were there and it was easy to carry on with the friendships forged in our first few days on the other side of the world. In fact so many years later I am still in touch with two of them, Wendy Evans and Mary Strange, one Welsh and one Irish, both living in the south of England. Our lives have moved on now but we still have so many memories to share. I wonder if they still remember sitting by the swimming pool in Selerang listening to Tom Jones singing 'The Green Green Grass of Home' and actually feeling homesick?

I suppose we learned a fair amount in the three years that we spent on the other side of the world. It was certainly different to the wartime East and the army was much different to the present day set up. I suppose I was lucky that my husband had gone through the dangerous parts of his service before I met him and also that he had sowed most of his wild oats. Not all of them though. I recall a day just before Christmas when the Lifeguards had one of their mad rituals in the mess. The Brick Hanging was a ceremony that deserves a mention, as it was weird. It was a full day of drinking in the mess, basically. A brick was hung up by the bar and nobody was allowed to leave or stop drinking until it was taken down. It was a males only day in the mess and the wives had little drinking parties themselves that day but as most of us had children we had to watch our intake. I went to bed at a reasonable hour and fell asleep. The next thing I was being wakened by a scream from Lim, and a scream from Colin. He had come home in the early hours of the morning, taken off his clothes and was too drunk to get into bed, so he was lying stark naked on a mat by the door. Lim had stayed the night and had come into the bedroom with two cups of tea for us in the morning and got the fright of her life. She dropped the cups of tea and Colin got a splash which woke him up and he scrabbled into bed with the mat clutched round him. Poor Lim, she couldn't look at him for days. I got up and found an enormous carved teak fork and spoon propped by the bedroom door. A raffle prize which Colin had won and used to prop himself up sufficiently to walk home with his friends . . . across Snake Valley!

Chapter Five

AND SO IT ENDED, MY FIRST taste of the Far East: in a plane coming back with all my friends and two little boys who were very excited. Norman who had become a bit of a telly addict in Singapore got on to the plane and as I was doing his seat belt up he asked me, 'When do they start firing at us?' He had only seen people getting on planes in war movies and expected us to be under attack any minute. I don't know whether he was relieved or not when we assured him that there would be no guns firing at us. He was a very deep-thinking little boy.

I remember very little of the whole trip save a stopover in Dubai where we immediately felt the change in climate. It was freezing cold and I congratulated myself on having changed the boys into woollies in anticipation, until we got off the plane into a foot of dust. The boys were absolutely filthy and I spent most of our time in the airport cleaning them. It was the middle of the night so we saw very little of the country. The timing also meant that the airport lounge was on skeleton staff and could only offer us coffee and apples. The apples stuck in my mind as they were the biggest I have ever seen to this day. Bigger than many a good-sized turnip. We were very glad to get airborne again an hour after we were supposed to leave as the plane had something wrong with it, by this time the children had found the dust again but we mums just let them get on with it and cleaned them up when we eventually got back on board again.

It was a long, long flight and I did not sleep at all so it was a very welcome moment when we landed at Heathrow. Two of my brothers, Donald Angus and Donald John, met us and after having a coffee with them the three years since we had seen them just vanished. I was horrified to see that Donald John's hair was a good fifty per cent grey, but as both my mother and father had gone grey very young I guessed that we would all lose our hair colour fairly soon. After an hour or so with them we got the train to Bristol where we had a lovely welcome from all Colin's folk, including Ken and Beryl's baby, Rosalind, who had been born while we were abroad. She was gorgeous with big blue eyes and a head full of blonde curls and I think that the moment I saw her I wanted to have another go at producing a girl! There is a saying in the army that anyone who goes to the Far East comes back with either a camphor-wood chest or a baby. Well, I had bought the chest but despite being warned by the doctor not to have any more pregnancies I had decided to have another try. Thank you, Rosalind!

When we'd spent some time with Colin's family we went up to Scotland to visit mine and the boys were well and truly spoilt there. The years of growing up in the strong Malaysian sun had made their hair completely blonde and with their big blue eyes they were very good looking little boys. They were also still at the well-behaved stage that comes before school and so they were very popular with all friends, neighbours and of course their grandparents.

I noticed that my father had got a lot older looking and was also a bit quieter. I think the fact that he had brought up four boys and none of them had wanted to stay in Uist and work the croft was getting to him and was souring his outlook on life. However he made the most of us while we were there and of course we had a ceilidh with as many of the old gang there as he could muster. Poor old Willie Jordan, the Irish packman, who had come to Uist and stayed there for a lifetime of crossing swords and drinking with my father, had gone and he was much missed. His tales were still told and if he was anywhere near us at that time his wheezy chuckle must have been much in evidence. I can honestly say that I never heard anyone say a bad word about him since his death and there aren't many people who go to an adopted land and fit in so well. Perhaps it's the Uist way, I don't know.

Jean MacDonald, my old friend of yore was now living in the north of England and most of my old friends of my own age had got married and left. Still there were enough of the older crowd around and we had a quick trip to Benbecula to visit the cousins and Doug and Barbara Braid. Doug and Barbara had decided to stay in Benbecula long term and were looking to get some land and build a house there. The crofter's hands were still pretty much tied as regards selling off their land or even building a second house for one of their children. In fact although they had lived on the land for generations they were still only renting and had very little rights. They could work their crofts if they had the inclination or indeed the manpower but a lot of them were in the same situation as my father . . . much land and nobody to work it, and no right to build a house for one of their children to inhabit. No wonder the more forward-thinking of the younger generation made their homes in the cities and only came back to the islands when the laws changed.

The absence of his children soured my father's whole outlook on life and that was becoming evident during this visit. My mother was of a different nature. I suppose her role had always been more of a younger sister to the aunties; she had come back to the island at their request and so she could always depend on Aunty Catherine to bale her out if there was a financial necessity. My father was a much more independent type of character and when he could see that it was all getting too much for him that was the beginning of the end. He was still doing the odd concert and recording for the BBC but the younger crowd had taken over and time had moved on.

Still, a visit from the family, especially if the grand-children were there, would raise everybody's spirits and our return from Malaysia was very exciting for us all. Alick came home from Glasgow and it was a packed house. As we did not have our own car we were rather dependent on dad's car and so could not go off when we wanted to but time was short anyway so we 'did the visits', drank much tea and enjoyed a taste of the island once again.

My particular memory of that visit was meeting our neighbour John, complete with bike, outside our house, coming home from the shops. I rushed up and gave him a big kiss. Big mistake, he was so embarrassed that he could not look me in the eye and spoke to my toes all the time. When he was leaving he said, 'Don't become too English, or I won't know you.' So the kiss was wrong. Pity. He was getting older and had started to build a new house but seemed to have lost a lot of his zest for life. I mentioned it to my mother and she told me that he had had a big disappointment. He'd harboured false hopes of marrying a Barra girl who had been over visiting her sister. The sister was married to a local man. Most of the romance had been in poor John's head and when he arrived in Barra to claim his bride she laughed at him and sent him home. It takes a good while to get over that in a small village. Poor man.

The look of the land was changing slowly, there were many more new houses and a lot less cattle and peat stacks around. The roads were slightly better and there were many more cars even in Kilpheder. Women were no longer labelled as drunken wasters if they were seen in a bar and although Benbecula was still the main place for earning money, thanks to the army, a few local people had started up businesses. The shops had extended but were still under the same management and new business had to be vetted and sanctioned to the extent that many people didn't bother with all the fuss and were content to let the island's business empires go on pretty much as before.

Before we left we had a party. Our friends came from all over the place – much older people, as most of the generation I'd grown up with had left the island and it was winter, not the summertime when they would come back to visit their families. Still, a few drams and it was as good a party as I can remember. My father was still in good voice and gave us many a rendition of old songs and a few new ones, which, I suspect, were his own. As the winter was now well underway with every other day a wet one, much of the talk was about winter pastimes and Colin was given a good grounding in the Uist traditions that night. How much of it is true and how much is tainted by my memory I can not say , but I will write it as I recall it, this is what they told him:

In parts of North Uist and other islands of the Hebrides the New Year is celebrated on the 12th day of 'Am Faollach' (January – The Season of the Wolf), probably a pre-Christian and certainly a non-Catholic event. 'Oidche Chullaig' is also peculiar to the Hebrides although someone in the gathering had heard of a similar ritual in the south of England called 'Wozzeling Night'. Both events involve adolescent boys each in their own village. The boys band together and armed with sacks go from house to house accepting offerings of bread and other items from the larder. Should a house be visited where there are no children the English wozzellers leave a piece of bread there. I don't think anyone could remember the origin of this ritual which took place on the last day of the year and it amazed me how many of the older members of the company could recite the 'Duan' although even then the practice was dying out. The men were particularly proud of their expertise although if they couldn't remember a line the women invariably prompted them. I have mentioned this particular Duan in a previous book and have had many enquiries about it, so here is the complete version as recorded in Brae Lynne so many years ago. Please note that it says '. . . *se maireach latha Nollaig*' (tomorrow is Christmas Day), which is a bit odd as it was recited on Hogmanay:

Tha mise nochd a dol air Chullaig
A dh'urachadh dhuibh na Callaig
A dh'innse do mhathan a bhaile

Gur e maireach latha Nollaig
Cha ruig mi leas a bhi ga innse
Bha e ann bho linn mo sheanar
Direadh aig an ard dorus
a tearnadh aig an dorus
dhuan a ghabhail aig a chomhlaidh
Modhail eolach mar is aithne
Cassain callaig tha na m' phocaid
Is math an ceo thig as an fhear ud
Beiridh fear an tighe na dorn air
Stobaidh e a'shron anns an teallach
Thig e dieseil air na paisdean
Is gu h-araid air bean an tighe
Bean an tighe is fhearr is dioch
S e a' lamh a riarachadh nam bonnach
Ma tha e agad 's an t-saoghal
Ma dh'fhaodas tu na cum mail orm
Tha mise teachdaireachd Mic De
Fosgail, fosgail lig a stigh mi!

Tonight I go about the duty of Cullaig
To renew the celebration of Callaig
To tell the wives of the township
That tomorrow is Christmas Day
I do not need to remind you
It's been so since my Grandfather's day
Climbing up the lintels
And descending at the door
Saying my poem outside the entrance
Respectfully, knowledgeably as I know how
In my pocket there is a Callaig candle
Which will produce much smoke
The man of the house will take it
And will put its tip into the fire

He will take it round the children
And especially the woman of the house
The housewife is most worthy
Her hand is giving out the bread
If you have it in this world
If you can, do not detain me
I am here with instruction from God's son
Open, open let me in.

When the boys had their bread and went on to the next house they would shout 'A Chullaig a Challaig Hello!' loosely translated as 'It's Cullaig it's Callaig Hello!' and I can remember hearing this in my childhood. Also their farewell to the house as they left, '*Ma se 'hearr a nochd gum a seachd searr bliadhn' o nochd!*' (If it is good tonight may it be seven times as good a year from tonight!'). I believe that the Duan varied in different islands and also this is only one of the many but seemed to be the most popular in Uist. It was an intriguing mixture of pagan ritual and Christian insets so it must date from way back.

Another bleary eyed departure from Uist, and we felt that we'd never been away. I remember wearing a suede coat with at least three jumpers on to keep out the cold. When I got more acclimatised the coat was far too big for me but came in handy as a maternity covering as I had decided that whatever the doctors had said I was going to try and produce a girl. So, shortly after we rejoined the regiment in Towyn, North Wales I was pregnant. John and Wendy Evans were there and Ken and Mary Strange but as happens with regiments a lot of our friends from Malaysia had been posted out to various other places.

Towyn was a nice place but the Welsh ignored us, so we were very much dependent on each other. It was a good job that we had been pretty isolated from the Malays and Chinese during our Far East posting as it was good training for Wales. We had very nice bungalows practically on the beach, which was lovely in the summer but there was a winter to get through first. I have never been so cold in my life! It didn't matter that I was by now pregnant or that I kept a good fire going all the time I just couldn't get acclimatised to the Welsh winter. The children were fine: Norman had started school, Philip had a little nursery school which he attended in the mornings and if they missed the swimming pool and the lovely weather of the Far East they didn't mention it. Their hair darkened slowly and the beautiful tans faded but they were healthy and happy and looking forward to having a girl baby in the house. I kept telling them that it might be another boy but they always gave me the same answer, 'Have the girl first, mummy, then you can have another boy.'

It was quite easy for our families to visit us and there were many weekends when we had a full house, so the days fairly flew by. I spent the entire time wearing two or three sets of clothes to keep warm and worked very hard in the house to try and keep my temperature up, so the place was as clean as any house I have ever had. The pregnancy went well although our parish priest got a couple of frights along the way. Once I was up a ladder cleaning the windows and he came up behind me and said, 'Mrs Hall, you shouldn't be doing that in your condition.' I promptly fell off the ladder. Since I had fallen on top of him I think he was in a much worse state than I was. Another day he was passing by and called out to me and I turned to answer him and fell over a bucket. By this time I think he was past caring what happened to me.

Well, December came and the decorations were up and on the thirteenth we got our little girl, Colin got promoted and he bought a new car. So ever since then the thirteenth has been regarded by us as a lucky day. Shona was a lovely baby, much wanted by all the family, and I breathed a big sigh of relief. Unfortunately, my body was not too happy at having to deliver another baby and the doctor said that I'd have to have a hysterectomy straight away. I persuaded him to wait a while and see if things got better and he agreed. My friend, Mary Strange, was in the hospital at the same time as me as her little girl, Catherine, had meningitis and she turned the corner the night Shona was born, so we were both happy.

After a short time another posting came through for Colin – an English one in Malvern at the Royal Radar Establishment and we said goodbye to Wales and our friends from the Far East trip and made our way up-country to Malvern. Colin's service time was coming to an end and it was likely that this would be his last posting so now we could look forward to buying a house and settling down. Ha Ha! But more of that later.

We arrived in Malvern and were given a nice married quarter, a semi-detached bungalow in Malvern Wells. The house was nice but the situation was not. There was a hill practically in front of it and every morning when I looked out of the window the hill seemed to say, 'This is the end of the earth'. I was deeply depressed by it, but my state of mind had a more sinister cause. The hysterectomy which had been recommended after Shona's birth had not yet been done and I was a medical mess. The doctor in Wales had written to the one in Malvern and had told him all the facts but the Malvern doctor had a streak of anti-army madness. He told me that he had so many army wives coming to ask for hysterectomies because they were too mean to buy the birth control pills, and that I was probably one of them, so I would have to have a full examination before he could sanction any treatment. Fortunately for me there was a cancellation in the hospital and my examination was brought forward. The result was that I was rushed into hospital the following day, and after a bungled operation where I was given an anesthetic to which I was allergic and following other minor mishaps, was kept in hospital a bit longer than we expected. Then I was sent to a lovely mansion type house to recuperate for a week and at last I was allowed to go home.

The boys had been looked after by my mother-in-law but Shona was given to my sister-in-law Beryl to care for. She brought her into the hospital to see me and put her down on the foot of the bed. Shona gave me a big smile and crawled all the way up the bed to give me a kiss. That was the first time I had seen her crawling and I'll never forget it. I had a home-help allocated to me by the Health Board for a month after my operation, but I'm afraid that the fear of being found with a dirty house which I had acquired with the various moves we'd made meant that I got up and cleaned before she came each morning. She was a nice old lady and drank numerous cups of black tea while she gave me the news of people I had never heard of before, from outside the camp. There was a boy she did the housework for whose parents had split up and he looked after his mother, who had had a 'brain scuttle' as she called it. The boy was working but from what she told me his own brain didn't seem too healthy. There were a few old ladies that she did shopping for and me, whom she called 'my army lady'. I don't think she could make me out and kept telling me to sit down and rest, but as soon as I sat down she'd sit opposite me and embark on another tale of woe. To tell you the truth I was glad to see the back of her.

Norman had slotted into his new school in Malvern Wells and went there on the bus every day. Philip was attending the camp playschool and Shona was being spoilt rotten by everybody. She was a lovely child, into everything but with such a sunny temperament that you could not be cross with her. Even if her birth had cost me more than a few weeks in hospital I would have considered her well worth the effort. I took her out for walks and gradually got to half-like Malvern Wells as all the women were very friendly, if a bit older. In fact Shona was the only baby in our road and everybody's pet.

Colin was away for three days every week at EMI in Hayes, Middlesex and came home with many a tale mostly about his travelling companion, a captain called Mick Moran. Mick had been commissioned from the ranks and they got on really well. You were supposed to observe a complete occlusion zone between the ranks of officers and men as they called it. If your best friend became an officer you had to call him sir and more or less ignore him. Well, I've never been too fond of tugging my forelock and neither has Colin, especially as he had refused to become an officer several times, right from the day he finished at Marling School in Stroud and was told to go to Sandhurst to the Officer's Training School. His mother could not afford the considerable financial outlay and so he went into the Army Apprentices School and on to REME learning trades instead. His promotions were quick and it was a good move as he has never been out of work and never had to kow-tow to anybody.

Mick had been a late baby and by the time he had

grown up his parents were pretty old. He was very accident-prone and so were they so some of his stories were hilarious. I particularly remember Colin coming home and telling me of the time when Mick had been visiting his parents and his father was not feeling very well so he decided to take him to the doctors for a check up. Unfortunately, he found that the car had a flat tyre and he told his dad to get ready to go to the doctor as he went to change the tyre on his car.

He took the wheel off and was about to put the spare wheel on when the main bolt rolled away and as he watched it rolled along the road and into a deep crack. He tried and tried to get it out but couldn't and every time he fished at the thing it went deeper and deeper into the crack until it eventually disappeared. By this time his dad was getting very grumpy so he decided to call an ambulance and take him to the hospital instead of the doctor's as there was a surgery there for elderly patients. The ambulance came and off they went. On the way to the hospital the ambulance crashed and his dad's stretcher shot out of the back and on to the street and he ended up with two broken arms. I know it's not a laughing matter but the tale went on and on to him coming home and digging up half the road to try and find the bolt to fix his car wheel and eventually fishing out a broken beer bottle top. The bolt was safe and sound under the car all the time.

I can recall visiting them one evening and the whole house seemed to be full of piles of linen. We didn't say anything but Margaret, Mick's wife, kept bursting out laughing and eventually he told us what had happened. She had sent him up to the loft to bring down a tablecloth. He got the cloth and was bringing it across the loft to the trap door when he slipped and put his foot through the ceiling. In trying to repair the damage he caused a leak in the cold water pipe and she had to take all her stored linen down until the plumber came to repair it. Nothing that Mick touched ever seemed to be safe. The last we heard of him he'd bought a lovely old bungalow and was renovating it himself. He had started by putting a floor to ceiling window in the lounge and his dog had been through the glass twice.

It did not seem to matter that I was on my own for half the week as I was kept busy with the children and Colin always brought something back from Hayes for us. He was doing a course in business management at the college in his spare time so he had no worries about getting bored. One weekend however he was definitely not himself, full of aches and pains and with a bad throat, so on the Monday morning I got Norman off to school, Philip off to nursery and got the car out to take Colin to the doctor. Shona was in the car-seat and her pushchair was in the boot.

It was flu so, armed with a prescription, we made for the chemists which was at the top of a hill on the way into Malvern Wells past the large field where the Three Counties Show is held. I mention this field because we were just passing it when the car ran out of petrol. My fault completely. I should have filled up before leaving the camp as it was Monday morning and Colin had driven home on Friday night emptying the tank and had been sick in bed all weekend. My fault, no question. Huh.

So Colin took Shona in the pushchair and his medicines and set off to walk the mile or so home while I walked up the hill to Malvern Wells petrol station to get petrol for the car. I was hoping for a lift but not one car passed along the road that morning and the same fate befell me on the way back. I particularly remember that I was wearing a pair of newish boots that were crippling me. However I breathed a sigh of relief when I got to the car and started to take the petrol cap off. It wouldn't budge. I tried and tried and I couldn't make the darned thing move. I was sitting by the car hitting the petrol tank lid with a stone and crying my eyes out when a dear old man drove up, stopped and said, 'Whatever is the matter, my dear?' I sobbed out my story and he got a tool-case out of his car and after a few tries the lid was off and the petrol was in the car and the sun shone again. 'Where do you come from?' the man asked. 'South Uist,' I replied. It was only later as I thought about the look of utter astonishment on his face that I realized that the poor man just wanted to know where I had come from that morning. By the time I had taken the container back to the garage and driven home it was a good three hours since Colin had begun his trek homewards and I was comforted by the fact that he would be warmly sitting by the fire having settled Shona and taken his medicine.

Not so, when I pulled up outside the house I was surprised to find that they were both still outside. Colin had spent two hours in the coal shed, with Shona in the pushchair happily playing with coal and black as the ace of spades. He was trying to light a cigarette with the soldering iron and the key to the house was on the dashboard of my car. Oh dear.

Chapter Six

SO LIFE WENT ON. Colin made the garden look present-
able and the children played out there when the
weather got better. We were also having family visitors
quite regularly. Colin's niece, Julie, came and spent a
week with us, much to the excitement of Mick Moran's
son who took her to the pictures. Alas, I feel that Julie
was a bit disappointed in the date as there was no repeat
episode. We enjoyed her company. I missed Wendy and
Mary and all the friends whom I had left in Wales but at
least the weather was much warmer and I soon made new
friends. As Colin already knew many of the soldiers it
was easy for me to slot into the wives' company and we
were that bit nearer our families so visitors were always
coming.

Colin was happy in his work and the children kept me
going and although I still had to be careful not to lift
anything heavy or do any stretching for a while I felt
great. The mess life was good and babysitters no problem
so apart from the dark forbidding hills which seemed to

come in through the lounge window it wasn't a bad time in our lives.

We had very good friends particularly Lew and Fran Birt who had been friends of Colin's from way, way back. They had bought their own house and urged Colin to do the same. Things were changing in the army. The rent for married quarters had shot up dramatically and Colin decided that as we were within three and a bit years of his leaving the service we ought to take their advice and look for a house of our own. The hills were still bearing down on our lounge window so I was in full agreement to his plan. Our mortgage repayments on a nice house would actually be less than the army rent so we went a house-hunting.

We found a lovely house in Malvern Link a few miles away. Detached with a three-quarter-acre garden. It was a modern three bedroomed house and was lived in by an old lady and her husband who was a keen if rather old-fashioned gardener. The front garden was full of the most beautiful rose bushes and the back was a half acre which was good 70 per cent vegetables. The old man had killed every sparrow that dared to come into his garden so he wasn't my type of person but the hills were well away and I was ecstatic! The price . . . £5,000!! It seems almost unbelievable now but that was the state of the market then. We had no complaints. A friend of ours, Harry Grey, had left the army and lived with his wife and three children just up the road from us. He really like the neighbourhood so that was an added advantage. They had a little daughter and she and Shona got on very well.

So, without further ado, we bought the property and moved in. Colin and his brother Ken did a bit of decorating but the biggest job was the back garden. They planted a hedge of trees right round it, replacing the wire net fencing, and got rid of the vegetables, which made it look like a market garden. The ground sloped away from the house so they terraced it, laid two lawns, planted flowers and generally made it all look completely different. Hard work but definitely worth while. There was a sand pit for the children to dig in and enough space for all their friends to come round and play so we were well happy.

A good primary school stood at the top of our road within easy walking distance for Norman, and Philip was now eligible so that was them sorted. If we could get a nice lady to come and look after Shona I could try and get back to teaching again. So I advertised in the local shops and got plenty of interest. Shona wasn't very taken with any of the applicants until a certain red-haired lady called Mrs Drabble turned up and it was love at first sight. I gave her a cup of tea and a biscuit and Shona helped herself to a biscuit, went over to Mrs Drabble and said, 'Hello Dabble' and dipped her biscuit in 'Dabble's' cup. So began a great love affair and to this day many years later we are in touch with Mrs Drabble.

The boys soon gathered a gang of friends round them and I got a job at the Grove Infants School in Malvern Link a few miles away. The weeks sped by and the weekends were full of activities. We walked the Malvern hills with our little brood and Shona loved to pick the flowers especially the purple-headed foxgloves which she put one on each finger and ran around shouting, 'Yah! I am a fox, look at my gloves!'. One day the boys and their father had strayed far ahead of us when we heard loud cries coming towards us and Norman, running as fast as a young deer, came into sight laughing his head off. He was closely followed by Philip and Colin and a huge formation of wasps clustered round Philip's head. Colin was beating at them and Philip was screaming 'Get them off me, get them off me!' Well Colin got them off him and suffered a few stings himself in the transaction but poor Philip had so many stings that it took a whole bottle of Calamine lotion to calm him down. However he was lucky, the next morning the swellings had gone down and he had no further trouble apart from a very healthy regard for wasps. A few weeks later our friend Harry Grey got stung by a wasp just above his left eye and had to go to hospital as he was allergic to wasp stings so he wasn't so lucky.

Mrs Drabble and Shona got on famously and there were very few days that there were any problems to report when I came home. However, one day was different. Shona had been a bit restless the previous night and was falling asleep the next morning so Mrs Drabble decided to put her in her bed for a nap. As she settled her down the bedroom door slammed and try as she may Mrs Drabble couldn't open it when she wanted to come back down stairs. She waited for a while and then she heard the postman coming through the front gate so she opened the window and called, 'I'm locked in here.' The postman, a very agile and fast-moving young man, called out, 'Never mind, I'll leave the parcel on the step', and shot off! Fortunately the milkman was a bit more helpful and he came in and opened the door from the outside for her.

During our time at this house the Canadians came for a visit again. We took them up the hills and they liked the house and we really enjoyed having them. I can remember making a beef stew for their dinner and cooking a chicken to have for a salad the next day. After they had finished their meal I went out to the kitchen to wash up and two of the Canadian boys were out there finishing off the chicken which they had found in the fridge! Obviously not enough stew.

Each summer we went to the Three Counties Fair and walked around marvelling at the beautiful flowers and enormous cattle. We always managed to lose at least one child so a large part of the day would be spent frantically looking for the missing person. In those days the world wasn't such a dangerous place for children and we were not particularly worried about their safety but always breathed a sigh of relief when we found them watching a wrestling match, having their faces painted or in Shona's case looking at a flower arranger doing her work.

We visited the Hebrides for our summer fortnight and had the usual late nights. The boys were just the right age for my father to spoil and he took them fishing and over to the machair to play on the beach. Philip was forever questioning him about this and that and he was very patient. My brother Alick was visiting at the same time one year and he had just had a very frightening experience, a brain hemorrhage which had given us all a fright. Fortunately he had recovered but was a lot quieter and more introspective. On the ceilidh night he read a poem which he had just written and I shall never forget it:

Childhood Memories

The clock on the mantelpiece ten minutes fast,
The shoes to be mended with leather and last,
'Oh look there's a stranger – he's asking the way.'
All things that remind me of long ago days.
The stout cardboard boxes in print EGGS WITH CARE
You sent them by post and they always got there,
Sacks of grain for the hens, was it called Kepple Maize?
All parcel and part of these long ago days.

On the bench there was lino, and sand on the floor,
No need to be bothered to lock up a door,
Why? Visitor's news might be coming your way,
To brighten the nights of the long ago days.
Old Mary would come with her knitting and shawl,
She'd call from the lobby, 'It's me after all!'
All the neighbours in turn she'd decry or would praise,
As we talked through the nights of these long ago days.
A.C. and the Co-op brought shops to your door,
As for tick – that was private and nobody saw,
You could still raise your head as the van drove away,
But that was back then in those long ago days.
Our cuddly toys were real dogs and cats,
They weren't just there for the mice and the rats,
No collars or leads to restrict them in play,
With their friends, not their masters in long ago days.
All the Scots and the Sandys, wee Cindy and George,
Tom Dooley and Rex from the large to the small,
They were part of our family, for part of the way,
All there to put heart in the long ago days.

When they came out to visit, Dad walked the Malvern
Hills with us and always walked way ahead of us. To him
the hills were natural stamping ground and his easy
strides didn't falter as he hummed a Gaelic song to
himself. He was getting on in years but had stopped
drinking and seemed to be content.

About two years after we moved into our first house
we noticed that a house we had been looking at on
Alexandra Road, a bit further into Malvern Link, was up
for sale. It was an old house, very spacious and grand
looking and we'd been intrigued to find a brass plaque on
the gate saying that Sir Edward Elgar had lived there.
Well, the property boom was just about to start and as

we had not been in there very long we thought that £6,000 would be about right for our house so we put it on the market. However, Colin was in Manitoba doing cold weather trials on some equipment and I saw what was happening; I took the house off the market and put it back on for much more. We sold our £4,000 property for £12,500 overnight and bought Elgar's house.

It was a great old house altogether. The living accommodation was on four floors with a semi-basement which had been made into a large two bedroomed flat with its own entrance. Originally this would have been servants' quarters, I assume, but it had been modernised by the previous occupants. There was a large storeroom behind the kitchen in the basement and we discovered a huge well under cover at the back of it. It was dry in our time but when you dropped a stone in it took ages to reach the bottom. We later found out a lot of the house's history and discovered that Elgar had written his wonderful 'Enigma Variations' sitting on our top lawn.

It was a time for many renovations and Colin's brother Ken was much in evidence – he would come down for a few days, Colin would take time off work and the sawing and hammering would begin. I was even roped in and will always be able to erect a tongue and grooved wall if anybody needs me. They made a wonderful job of the house and I could see us still there when our grand-children came. The children were dog crazy and as we now seemed settled enough to consider having a puppy we decided to look for a nice small dog which we could all control and would not need too much space in the house during the day when we were all out. Somebody gave us the address of a breeder who had a kennel with some fine little Cavalier King Charles Spaniel puppies and we got a lovely little black and tan called Carlo. He was a beautiful little chap and so easy to manage. He slept for most of the time we were out and was full of energy when we came home, ready for walks, playing with the children and generally keeping us all in trim. When I came home from work I usually let myself in through the basement door and I could hear him coming to greet me from whichever room he was in, thundering down the five flights of stairs and skidding to a halt at my feet, usually dropping a ball or an old shoe as a welcome home present. We had a large wooden pet area in the garden with two fluffy guinea pigs and a rock house with a wandering tortoise in residence. I called him wandering because he had a habit of wandering out of the garden but as he always turned left when he got to the gate he wasn't too difficult to keep track of him.

At about this time we had a very sad thing happen. Our friend and near neighbour Harry Gray got up one morning, had his breakfast and picked up his car keys, kissed his wife goodbye and dropped dead. Needless to say we were all stunned as he was a fit man and had just turned forty. It took Joyce, his wife, a long time to get over the shock and we were all shocked by the realization that apparent good health is no real prediction of your lifespan. Joyce and her three children managed to cope but it was a sobering time for us all.

Colin's time in the army ended and he started work in the Civil Service in Worcester. He was not very happy there as he had to start off on a far lower pay scale than he had been used to and regarded it as a stopgap occupation while he looked for something better. I was very happy at my school and the job of Deputy Head was a possibility. Shona was attending a very posh kinder-garten and the boys were getting on fine at their school. Norman had expressed a keenness to learn the piano and so we found a lovely old Bluthner piano and got him started on lessons. We didn't have any inkling that he was really any good at music until his teacher entered him for the Worcester Music Festival and he came home with second prize. Philip then started and was also very musical, however the time spent practicing was frequently interrupted by other more enticing pastimes and sadly over the weeks the piano was neglected.

I had a nice little car for my job and Mrs Drabble had to leave us and was replaced by another equally nice lady Mrs Dodd, who took over the role of mum very well. She had worked in the canteen at my school so I knew her well and when Mrs Drabble had to leave she was very happy to step in and have a job closer to her home. She took Shona to kindergarten, came back, did the housework, met Shona when school was over, took her to her own house for lunch then did something nice with her for the afternoon and brought her to school to meet the boys and take them all home in time for me to come home from school. Oh, it was all going very well, too well maybe.

You may have noticed that there is little mention of Colin's new job any more. Well, he was getting a bit dissatisfied by the red tape and slowness of promotion prospects and generally was not too happy at his new place. I was getting a lot of nice things brought home from his shopping sprees at the Royal Worcester shop so I just bided my time and hoped that things would get better for him. So when he came home one day with a letter offering him a new job I was surprised but happy, until I realized that the job was in Johannesburg!

Reading this now I realize that I must have been mad, completely cuckoo, but something inside me said, 'GO'. A chance to see South Africa, good schools for the children and a house with a swimming pool were part of the package, it was an eighteen-month renewable contract, and the pay was very good too. We went up to London to talk to the Atlas Aircraft Company representative who gave Colin an interview and completely sold me on all the lovely houses and facilities and so we decided to have another move. Now, you must remember that this was in 1974 and South Africa was then a white dominated country and still a place where apartheid ruled so this gave us a few uncomfortable thoughts, but we decided that eighteen months would be time enough for us to decide whether we wanted to stay there or come back home. The British way of life wasn't too great at the time and we felt that a change could do us no harm. Worcestershire was a great place but there was little prospect of a decent job for Colin and the children would have to leave to get work when the time came for them to join the workforce and so we decided that it was an opportunity not to be missed.

Colin's family were supportive as were mine. They had all got used to Colin moving around a lot in the army and were glad that we had got into the property market when we did and would have a good bit of money to take with us. When we came back we could buy another house. The children were not at all put out and were madly excited about going on a liner and seeing wild animals and snakes. I had my own thoughts about snakes but kept quiet about them for the time being.

The staff at my lovely primary school were all amazed but understood when I told them of our plans and arranged some great surprise gifts for me, mostly Royal Worcester pottery that I cherish to this day. I was deluged with presents from the children and parents, they were such nice people. We quickly sold our lovely house, had two great farewell parties and a goodbye trip to the Hebrides, and then it was back to sell the furniture and pack our worldly goods once again. On our last night in the house whilst the children were being looked after in Bristol we were feeling quite emotional and sitting in an empty lounge with no TV or anything else when there was a knock on the door and there were two of our friends from Malvern, Pat and Charlie Courage, complete with a bottle of whiskey and four glasses . . . I don't remember much else of that night. Next morning we picked the children up and were on our way to Southampton docks to board the *Pendennis Castle* before I had time to think. We boarded straight away and put Carlo into the hands of the Pet Steward. We were shown our sleeping berths in three lovely spacious rooms, (Shona had one to herself which she rarely used as she preferred to bunk in with us!) As the lovely liner pulled out of Southampton and the busload of relatives who lined the docks shouted and waved and the band played 'Auld Lang Syne' I felt a little sad but also very excited.

Chapter Seven

OUR FIRST PRIORITY AFTER GETTING ourselves settled into our palatial surroundings was to find out if any other new employees of Atlas Aircraft Company were among the passengers, and soon we got to know that there were two couples with their children also bound for Johannesburg and Atlas. We were a bit taken aback by the appearance of one couple who were dressed as if they were going on a very low budget package tour. The woman wore a tweed coat and a large Spanish style straw sun hat. She yelled at her two children in a strong Liverpudlian accent. The other couple was more like us and also had two children. By their accents we thought that the woman came from Bristol, and we were right. It came home to me that this would not be like the army foreign tours when we had always travelled and lived with people who were from a similar educational background, welcome to real life! I suddenly realized how very protected we had been with the army, true I had always followed my own career but with Colin's work always having been in the upper ranks of the service all my friends and the children's friends had been pretty much the same as us. I must admit that I felt a bit scared of the future.

However the voyage was wonderful. After leaving the wintry seas of the British Isles behind and surviving the dreadful Bay of Biscay, where my memories are of all the children piled into our cabin being seasick and frightened, feeling pretty awful myself and trying to act as normal on the second day by taking them to the cinema where *Bonnie and Clyde* was being shown to about six stalwart passengers. About halfway through the film the ship took an almighty dive and we were all thrown off our seats, rapid exit Hall family. I have yet to see the end of that film but have heard that the ending is pretty gruesome so perhaps the weather did me a favour.

Then the glorious sun came out and the rest of the voyage was marvellous. The boys had their own agenda as they were taken care of and pampered by special stewards in the children's entertainment area so we were left with only Shona who was a very obliging little girl and no trouble at all. When we stopped at Tenerife we all went round the island on a bus and the guide pointed out all the TV aerials. As people had just started to go there for their holidays there wasn't anything like the built up holiday hotels of today. It was quite a boring place, I thought and was glad to get back onto the ship and sail off once again.

The boys were well into the games they played on-board and were delighted to be taken round to the captain's deck and have their photo taken steering the ship. One of the entertainment stewards would come and take Shona if there was a special event which she would enjoy and we knew that she was perfectly safe. We spent the days sunbathing, watching whales and flying fish and taking part in the games which were organized for us by the entertainments officers. Of course we were intrigued by the grand ceremony that marked 'Crossing the Line' as we crossed the equator. As we had already crossed the equator twice by plane we were not made to take part in it but watched from the gallery. When I saw the people who had been invited to meet 'Neptune' being covered in shaving foam and practically flung overboard I was very glad that we were not his honoured guests.

Every evening we dressed up like royalty for dinner served by immaculately dressed waiters in a dining room full of stiff white tablecloths and silver. The children had their own dinner served earlier but we preferred that ours should eat with us and this was perfectly acceptable. At the end of the voyage many people came up to congratulate us on our well-behaved family. We didn't think that they were in any way out of the ordinary but there you are. The boys were quite able swimmers and spent a lot of the days in the swimming pool and Shona, not to be outdone, gave us the slip a few times and jumped in. Of course she couldn't swim and just held her hand up when she bobbed to the surface for one of the lifeguards to haul her out, laughing. By the time we docked she was able to keep herself afloat. I have done many cruises later on in life but not one will ever eclipse the time I spent on the *Pendennis Castle* between Southampton and the Cape of Good Hope. Sheer luxury. I believe that was the last time that the good ship sailed that voyage as shortly after that all the sailings were stopped and I am so glad that we were able to be part of the final company.

On the morning we arrived I was absolutely amazed at our first sight of Cape Town, from the sea. The sun was just coming up and magnificent Table Mountain was a brilliant pink. Below it stretched really palatial houses and the whole scene was like a film set. Breakfast was being served, I was rushing to finish so that I could go up on deck to see our new country and I broke a tooth. After traveling 6,000 miles by sea I wasn't going to let a small thing like that spoil my day.

When we disembarked at Cape Town we were reunited with our little dog and he seemed to take it all in his stride. He had spent two weeks on the dog deck with another dog for company and every morning Colin had to get up early before the decks were washed and walk him. He was delighted to see the children again and seemed to enjoy the sunshine on his back. After the usual formalities we were met by an uncle of Colin's, Bill Hopes, who had emigrated to Cape Town many years before and he took us home with him as our train to Johannesburg was leaving in the evening. He was so excited to have some of his family to talk to. He had a lovely house and he, his wife and his son were really hospitable to us. In the evening before we went to the station he drove us around Cape Town and showed us the other side of the gilded coin. I'll never forget the horror of seeing the black villages. The houses looked like heaps of rubbish: cardboard boxes, and old tyres piled up to make the walls and cardboard roofs. There were fires outside with children and dogs playing among the rubbish. Not a mile away the grand houses of the white folk suddenly seemed like a sin against humanity. However it was not my place to express this feeling then and we said our goodbyes to Bill and got on the train as we had another thousand miles to travel to get to Johannesburg.

By this time we had all really had enough of travelling and the Great Karoo, which seemed to go on forever, was very boring. Occasionally, we stopped and Colin dashed out with Carlo to let him do his business and obliging little dog that he was he always did it quickly and jumped back on the train. There was another English lady on the train with her dog and she and Colin always had the same conversation as they tended their dogs, 'Hello, another fine day isn't it?' At night we pulled the bunks down and slept as well as we could and we were very thankful indeed when we eventually arrived at Johannesburg after three days.

This might be a good time to outline the South Africa of 1974, the year we went there, as it was pretty different to the South Africa of today. Although it was not the place of eternal sunshine and untold riches for any white immigrant that it had been in years gone by, it was still pretty good for the white man. There was a white President Mr B.J. Vorster and the policy of apartheid was very much in place. For the whites there was absolutely no difference made to your social status according to your job, it was easy I suppose as the black workforce, for a miserable pittance, did all the menial jobs. The whites lived in grand houses, mostly with swimming pools, and black gardeners keeping their half or full acre immaculate. The back population were separated from the whites and lived in 'townships' in varying degrees of squalor. Apart from working in the white area for which a permit was required, 'never the twain shall meet'. Well, we all know what happened to that idea.

At the time we lived in South Africa it was a wonderful place for whites as long as you put thinking on hold. Think about the future and you thanked God that you had a British passport and that you and your family could go home before the boys were sent to the border to fight. The white population was made up of Afrikaaners, descended from the original Boer immigrants, and 'Rooinecks' the name given by the Afrikaaners to the descendants of the British immigrants, a derisory term relating to their sunburnt necks. The population also included Indians and Malays who were the descendants of immigrants and lived in their own villages, bound by the apartheid rules and used the non-white entrances, staircases, toilet facilities etc. There were black trains and white trains and buses and segregation even applied on the beaches. I once went up a 'Blacks Only' staircase by mistake and an old black woman shouted at me 'Nie blank, nie blank'. (Non whites), gesturing at the notice and I made my way back very smartly. It was a strange way to live coming from South Uist where the coloured packmen were treated like visiting royalty. During our time in South Africa changes were in the air but more of that later.

At the station we were met by an Afrikaaner in a minibus who drove us to a nice hotel in Kempton Park and told us that we would be shown the available houses the next day. Boy! It was so good to stop moving and to be able to close the door and have some peace and quiet. The children soon found the swimming pool and were content. Shona, jumped in, sank and held her hand up, unfortunately this was not the ship and there was no friendly steward watching her and she was going down for the third time when one of her brothers noticed and pulled her out. She has always been fearless and has had the most gruesome hobbies like potholing so I suppose the swimming was an early warning of things to come.

On the second morning Colin and the other two men whom we had met on the boat bound for Atlas went off to work and I sat with the wives looking at the housing papers and did a bit of exploring and window shopping

LEFT.
DONALD JOHN MACMILLAN
DIED 1985 AGED 48

ABOVE.
DONALD ANGUS MACMILLAN
DIED 2002 AGED 66

LEFT.
ALICK IAN MACMILLAN
DIED 2002 AGED 57

I no longer fear death, as I'm sure we will be together some day

LEFT.
Donald John was Special Branch bodyguard to Edward Heath and Harold Wilson

MIDDLE.
Just a Sunday evening with aunties and neighbours

BOTTOM.
Family funeral, Benbecula, c. 1900.

LEFT.
My first ever photo, with D.A and D.J.
and Benbecula grandparents, roughly
sixty-five years ago. I am the fat doll.

MIDDLE.
Our house in Malaya was on the edge
of the jungle

BOTTOM.
We travelled to Kuala Lumpur railway
station. A magnificent building.

LEFT.
The mosques were beautiful
and glittered with gold

BELOW.
Our house in Selarang
barracks was once part of
Changi Jail

RIGHT.
The snakes were everywhere,
even in the flower-pots

LEFT.
We bought Sir Edward Elgar's house. He composed the *Enigma Variations* on our front lawn.

BELOW.
Philip, Shona and Norman were delighted at the thought of another adventure, this time in Africa

TOP.
At Sudwala Caves we slept in Rondavels

ABOVE LEFT.
A large brown fierce one kept the others in line

ABOVE RIGHT.
Colin tested the boat by floating it on the swimming pool

TOP.
Beautiful Niagara, always
breathtaking

ABOVE.
The American presidents
captured in rock

LEFT.
The River Roy flows by
our house

ABOVE.
The beautiful
mountains that I see
every day

RIGHT.
My health improves and
I get older and wiser

with the children. We would be given a house to rent but it would be unfurnished so we had to find out where to buy beds etc pretty quickly. In no time at all the day was over and the men came back with the news that the company who had hired them – an American/British – concern had sold Atlas Aircraft to the South African government and had already moved out. It was all a bit chaotic. The younger of the other two men Alan Clayton, an engineer, had spent most of the day sweeping the floor. I really didn't know what we had gone into and was a bit despondent, but the contract, pay, and everything else was agreed before the takeover and was being honoured so we were at least protected in that way.

We had already decided that we would buy a house and invest our money, as living in rented accommodation can soon whittle your capital away. So we got a rented house in Impala Park as a temporary measure and bought furniture, curtains and the bare minimum of stuff to do us for the time being. Our little dog Carlo started off being very interested in his new home and ran round the garden playing his little games for the first few days then he began to get very listless and would not eat or play and just got thinner and ill looking so we found out where the vet was and took him in for a check-up. Well, he had been bitten by a certain kind of tick and his blood had been poisoned. The vet said that he could possibly save him if he drained his blood and gave him a supply of fresh blood. We had a very anxious time waiting to see if he would survive the operation and he did. However, the vets said that it was vital that he eat well and regain his strength and this proved to be a big problem. Always a finicky eater he now refused to eat anything and we were beside ourselves with worry. Then someone said that we should get another dog to go for his food and that might make him eat, so the next day Colin came home from work with this tiny puppy, a cross between a Maltese Poodle and a Dachshund, an accidental mating of two pedigree dogs, the cutest thing on four legs. Carlo was interested but too ill to be bothered, until the puppy waddled over to his food dish . . . well that was it, Carlo immediately pushed the puppy out of the way and gobbled up his dinner. There was no turning back, and we now had two dogs. Carlo and Mandy.

Colin's work seemed to be going OK and the children were still on school holidays so we gradually settled in. The only thing we had to wait for was the arrival of our money from the UK and also the boxes of our belongings, which had come over on a cargo boat. All that arrived eventually and the customs had opened our boxes and re-packed them any old way. Suffice it to say that my sewing machine had a fine time among the beautiful crystal ware, which I had bought especially as a souvenir of my old country.

We found a house to buy in Bonaero Park Extension 1, which was a housing development halfway between Johannesburg and Pretoria. The children's school was close by and it was near the main road, handy for Colin's work, so we moved in and loved it. It was a sprawling bungalow with four bedrooms on half an acre of immaculate garden with a lovely patio and a fair sized swimming pool. Sigh! The kind of house we never could have afforded in Britain unless we won the lottery. At this stage we were both quite taken with the South African way of life and had decided to think about staying beyond the end of Colin's contract as there seemed to be no end of good jobs on offer and the UK was in the depths of a depression.

The children were very happy and had made new

friends. When school started they were a bit troubled by the early morning eight thirty commencement but delighted at the one thirty closure. There were clubs and activities that they could enrol in for the rest of the afternoon and soon they were all very busy. Shona had started school and was very quickly into ballet, drama and all sorts of other clubs, so they were all well occupied. They had their bikes, which they used to get anywhere they needed to go, plenty of friends and were pretty independent and so I started to feel slightly redundant. We had the maid to do all the work, as most of the population did, and the number of hours you could spend on hobbies and having coffee mornings by the pool were innumerable but soon got boring. I had my tooth fixed and a worrying medical problem (extreme unexplained tiredness) sorted out. It turned out that I was sensitive to the extreme altitude (we were 5,000 ft above sea level) and needed iron and vitamin B12 transfusions every six weeks. I can honestly say that after each treatment I felt better than ever in my life. When I returned to the UK the doctors pooh-poohed it and I can't say that I felt any worse without it, but then I suppose that living at a lower altitude did the business.

Although we didn't need the money I decided to look for a job. Most of the women worked and as I had worked all my life I really missed it. So my friend, Betty Whorley from Scotland, and I started to look for jobs. Teaching was out as you needed to have a degree in Afrikaans to apply so I had to think fast. I didn't want a shop job as it would mean working on Saturdays. Betty had done some office work so I thought I'd invent an office background and see how I got on. We had a few interviews and Betty quickly got fixed up as her typing was very good. My typing was absolutely nil words per minute so I took a bit longer to get a job but eventually I got one with a company which imported washing machines and supplied them to the mining companies.

I was a statistics clerk and it was great. I shared an office and as there was a spare typewriter in there I soon taught myself to type. After years of teaching I loved the informality of working with grown ups and our old Jewish boss Mr Sonnenberg was lovely. I shared the office with an Irish girl, Phil Raddie. She had worked for the UN in Northern Ireland and was very, very clever. However she had reached the highest position that a Catholic worker was allowed to aspire to in that country and had emigrated to further her children's career prospects. We had several discussions about South African politics and the future and she was adamant that whatever happened she would stay there forever as there was no life for her and her young family back in Ireland.

Colin's job seemed to be working out quite well and he had transferred to another part of the company in Olifantsfontein a bit closer to home. There he trade tested young apprentices on radar and radio and our social circle widened even further as he got to know some nice people among the staff. They were mostly either immigrants or their descendents. We were particularly friendly with Sid and Ann Hill and spent many long days and evenings out on their 'plot', a thirty-acre farmland complete with horses that the children rode and we enjoyed their boundless hospitality.

Sid was a great storyteller and I particularly remember the tale of the dog and the horse. Sid's horses were all very highly bred and well looked after. One in particular, his daughter's horse, was a bit skittish. Apparently one of his neighbour's dogs started coming over and chased this particular horse. The horse stood it for a while then he started to face up to the dog and give it a few kicks. This escalated into a full-scale war until one day Sid went out in the morning and found the horse kicking a dead dog around the field. Well, Sid was not too friendly with his neighbour and he thought that the best thing to do would be to bury the dog and pretend to have no knowledge of its whereabouts if his neighbour asked about it. This was fine until the next morning when Sid went out and found that the horse had dug the dog up again and was kicking it around the field. Again and again he buried it and again and yet again the horse dug it up. Eventually Sid and his sons took the few remains that were left of the dog out on to a secluded corner of the veldt and buried it.

On the mantelpiece in their living room there was a glass jar full of strange looking bits of silver and one day I asked Sid what they were. 'Ach man,' he replied, 'that was my dog', and another tale unfolded. Sid had bought a very expensive gun dog with a view to breeding puppies and making a bit of extra cash. The dog was nice but had a habit of chasing cars. One day he chased a van and got run over very badly. Sid took him to the vet who said that practically every bone in his body was broken. It was what Sid had surmised and he said to the vet, 'Ach, well, man, you do the business.' Meaning put the dog down. Well, three weeks went by and Sid was wondering why he hadn't had a bill from the vet so he rang him up. 'You can come and get him now,' said the vet, 'I've made a good job of him and he will be fine if you just rest him for a while.' Sid was happy that the dog was all mended but a bit apprehensive when he thought about the bill. When he got to the vets surgery he was shocked to find that the vet had put silver pieces in the dog and his bill was more than the dog had cost originally. However a few days went by and the dog lay by the picture window getting stronger every day and Sid was thinking that all was well until one day the same truck came down the road and back-fired just before it got to Sid's house. The dog growled and shot through the window, injuring himself but paying no heed to that, he launched himself under the truck, end of dog. Well Sid was so incensed by all the bad luck he had that he dissected the dog and took all the silver bits back to the vet and asked for a refund. The vet refused to give him any money back and Sid put the jar full of bits on the mantelpiece to remind himself not to buy any more expensive dogs.

After we arrived in South Africa there was a long wait for letters from home and the telephone was not an option in those days as you had to wait for ages to have one connected. Even after we bought our own house we would really have to think twice before phoning to the UK as the tariff was extortionate. However after a while the mail caught up with us and we were in touch once again. My mother and father kept to their way of writing which had started when I was at school in Fort William, separate letters. There were also a good many tape recordings of evenings when the rest of the family were at home and sometimes just a tape recorded message from the two of them which often brought tears to my eyes. Colin's mother and brother were also good corre- spondents as was my brother Donald John, so we didn't feel too isolated. My sister-in-law Sheila had a job as a switchboard operator for the Metropolitan police and once we got a phone she found a way of connecting me to any one I wanted to talk to in the UK for no charge. This was good although it scared me to death as I had visions of being hauled back to England and charged with fraud. So I kept the illicit phone calls very short.

Most of the news from home was good but we were

very sad to hear that our neighbour's wife, Chrissie Mac-
Intyre, had died. I was devastated as we had been so
friendly and she had been very good to my parents. A
lovely young woman, she is still much missed. A brain
tumour was the cause and she had to endure much pain.
Poor Chrissie she will always be remembered kindly. Dad
was also sad to report that his little dog, Cindy, which
had been mine originally but had spurned me for my
father and went everywhere in the car with him had also
died. He wasn't going to have any more as he was so
upset, but somehow a few months later he reported that
he now had Sandy a cross between a large Collie and a
Border Collie, golden brown and white and the best dog
in the world. Ach, well . . .

Since moving to our house we had acquired some more
livestock of our own. There was a large brown and white
cat that belonged to the house whose name escapes me. I
was never a cat lover but this one was a very impersonal
sort of cat and it never bothered me. It left home in the
morning, came back in the evening, and slept in one of
the chairs in the kitchen after it was fed until it was
morning again and then off it would go. Colin built an
aviary in a corner of the garden and we had all kinds of
birds in there, cockatiels, love birds, budgies and some
little birds who didn't fly but just lived on the floor and
scampered around feeding and whistling. One of
Norman's school friends gave him a chicken which he put
in the aviary for one night. That was long enough for him
to eat half of the little floor birds so he was given away
swiftly.

Although we lived on a very civilized-looking estate
with manicured gardens there were many reminders that
we were not in Britain, snakes for instance. There were
not many ocassions when snakes came in the garden as

they don't really come looking for you and if one was there it was lost. However, Philip and, especially, Norman were snake mad and would often go out with their friends snake-hunting. I had forbidden this but as they grew older they got crafty and I would find a box in the garage with a suspicious scrabbling noise coming from it. They said that a teacher at the school bought the snakes from them and I made sure that they took the box to school with them. After many dire warnings they either stopped or got craftier about hiding the snakes and I saw no more for a long time.

We were very friendly with Betty and Derek Whorley whom I mentioned earlier and we often went to their house or they came to ours for a brai (barbecue). Their two daughters were older than our children but they would all swim happily together in the pool while we caught up with news from the UK and local gossip. Derek and Colin were both interested in sailing and as there was a very good sailing club about a mile away from us they decided to build boats and join the club. It was a big job and once the work was finished for the day the boat was hoisted up into the roof space in the garage until next time. One day I heard a lot of noise and some curses coming from the garage and found that Colin had somehow dropped the boat and smashed part of the base. Well, he managed to patch it up and eventually the boat was finished and painted a bright yellow and red and given the name *Brae Lynne* (My father's house name) in black. To make sure that it was seaworthy he and the boys carried it to the swimming pool and launched it. It was fine and we had a very merry evening with a bottle of wine afterwards with the children playing in the boat. From then on every Sunday was spent at the sailing club. Norman was a very able crew and he and Colin were always highly placed in the races and sometimes they won. Philip went out once. It was a very windy day and he proved that like me he hates sailing, at one stage his father was shouting 'Pull the sail in', and Philip was climbing up the mast and calling on God to save him. They capsized and I don't think Phil ever went in the boat again. Even Shona crewed for Colin once in a race. I don't think they were placed but everyone said 'Aaw!' when they docked and this tiny little girl got out and started pulling the boat up with her dad.

After we'd been in South Africa nearly a year we decided to go to Durban for a holiday. A friend of ours who had lived next door to Colin's brother in Bristol had emigrated a few years back and lived just outside Durban so we arranged to visit him, his wife and family. As we wanted to have some time on our own we rented a beautiful big house complete with servant near the Durban beach for a week. Shona brought her friend Melanie with her and we had a great time. The beach was beautiful and nearly deserted so we went down there every day and apart from the usual near death experience of the boys trying to drown themselves once or twice it was idyllic. The drive from Bonaero Park to Durban was pretty spectacular as the mountains we drove through were all shapes and colours. The roads were all great, in fact, I can safely say that the roads in South Africa were the best I've ever seen, from north to south, beautiful clean tarmacked roads and, apart from the morning and evening rush hours, almost deserted. Needless to say, on the way to Durban Colin got a speeding ticket.

We made contact with Cliff and Lil, the Bristol couple, and spent some afternoons at their house, which was very interesting as Cliff had just set up an antique business and I hate to say this but we spotted a few Cliff-made antiques among his stock. They had some dogs but one, a really pretty Pekinese called Chang, was a bit of a trial. He'd suddenly rush up and bite your leg, so we spent the time at their house with our legs tucked under us. One day we heard some strange noises coming from the garden and went to investigate. Shona and Melanie had made a shrine of flowers and sat Chang on the shrine. They were chanting, 'We worship you, oh Chang, heathen God.' And Chang was sitting there looking perplexed then he rushed at them and tried to get their legs. Each time he did this they caught him and tried again. This went on and on until in the end Chang was tired and fell asleep. The girls carried him in and said, 'He's cured now.' With that Chang woke up and bit them both. We enjoyed our trip to Durban very much and the city itself had a much more British feel to it than the Johannesburg area. Probably a lot more British ex-pats living there, I don't know. Cliff and Lil came up to visit us several times but left the dogs at home and I still have some lovely china that Cliff gave me from his shop.

Things were changing at my work and we heard that the company had been sold to a large South African group and they were bringing in all their own staff from managers down. It was a very sad time and we all cried a lot as it was such a friendly company and we could see that the managers were getting on in years and couldn't really rely on getting another job. We, the younger workforce, were practically guaranteed another job fairly soon but we felt for Mr Sonnenberg and the people who had started it all from scratch. They had taken on some new partners a few years previously and now they had been sidelined and sold off.

I quickly got another job with the catalogue company Greatermans in the office part of a large warehouse. My title was Office Manageress, which sounded very grand, but it was tedious work. Most of the office workers were Afrikaaners and not very friendly but I stuck at it and eventually got on the right side of them. I think. I did a bit of everything, and learnt to use the switchboard in my spare time. It was a strange place to work as sometimes there was just no work and then the vans would arrive from Johannesburg with so much paperwork that we were all flooded with it. But it passed the time and paid well.

One thing I did not like was that the only way I could get to the warehouse was by driving through a black township and although many of the people from the township worked in the factory part of Greatermans they were not friendly. If I passed any of the inhabitants when driving through they would spit on the ground and I always prayed that the car would not stall. I had never felt such hatred directed at me and it was not a pleasant feeling.

Chapter Eight

THE SOUTH AFRICAN GOVERNMENT WAS very unpopular overseas. Although Verwoerd, who was an ardent follower of the apartheid policy, had been assassinated his successor, B.J. Vorster, pursued the same policy of separate development as they called it. Well, it was separate all right but certainly not a fair deal for the black community. The Pass laws restricting the movement of black people within the country were causing international outrage. Thousands of the apartheid regime's opponents had been imprisoned without trial and more than 3,000,000 people had been 'resettled' in the black townships. This was not working as many of the blacks rebelled and moved around the country looking for work or plotting to overthrow the government that treated them so unfairly. Bishop Tutu was always heard preaching non-violent resistance to the apartheid laws and although the black people round us must have known about all this nothing really changed in their manner and we didn't feel too insecure. People around us said, 'Don't worry, we'll be alright, we're not South African', but I did wonder if your attacker would ask to see your passport before cutting your head off.

Colin left for Canada to attend his nephew's wedding and a day later serious unrest broke out all over South Africa. My first knowledge of it was having dirty big rocks thrown at my car as I drove through the township on my way to work. Once there we worked as usual but more than half the native workforce was missing. I was amazed at the attitude of the white South African workers, they relied completely on the government to sort everything out and said, 'This is our country, where are we to go? We must trust in the ones at the top.' I suppose they had a point. I had a convoy to escort me through the township on the way home and although we all stayed at home for the next day the trouble was all over in our corner of South Africa in twelve hours.

Colin enjoyed his Canadian trip although the wedding was cancelled. He made a lightning trip to England, to visit his mother, before coming home and we were glad to get fresh news of the folk at home. Colin's mother was in her late seventies and going blind so we were concerned about her. We decided to send her money to come out and spend Christmas with us and told her to bring any of her friends who wanted to come for company. Soon we had a very excited reply saying that she, her sister, and a friend whom we knew well would all be coming for a month just before Christmas. We offered to pay for my parents to come out too but they said that it was too far for them and would rather we used the money to pay for a trip back home to see them, so we promised to try and make it in the summer.

There was great excitement in our house waiting for Nana's visit. And all seemed to be going well until the children all produced spots the week before our people were due to arrive . . . chicken pox. The whole school was infected and there was nothing that we could do about it. The old ladies couldn't remember whether they'd had it or not and had bought their tickets so they decide to come anyway. So we had a whale of a time with them. Colin's mum had a problem as all her luggage was lost and turned up two days before she left, but we got her new clothes and she was happy. The children soon forgot about their spots and had plenty of Christmas presents and were delighted to have another lot when Nana's cases turned up. Auntie Flo was a brilliant seamstress and had brought me a length of beautiful rust-coloured fabric, which she made into a lovely evening dress for me in a few hours. I was the belle of the ball at a few parties, I can tell you.

By sheer chance our friends, Betty and Derek Whorley, had invited Betty's mother and father out at the same time, so we all got together several times and joined up for Christmas and New Year parties. We took our visitors all over the place, to Johannesburg and Pretoria, the Voortrekker monument and all the beautiful gardens and animal parks and had a good time ourselves. The only thing that grated was that Auntie Flo had had her first foreign holiday the year before . . . to Tenerife as it happened and if she said, 'When we was in Tenerife . . .' once she said it a hundred times. All too soon the visit was over and we promised faithfully to go home next year and saw them off at the airport tearfully.

I had been rather frightened by the trip through the African township when the riots were on and started looking for a job in another area where there wasn't so much danger of being stoned. One came up, near the airport, which was very tempting but as it was with an

American-British Company, Rank Xerox, I was a bit wary when I went for the interview. It was for statistics and computer programming and a bit of shipping. The company was huge and the workspace was palatial and I was very nervous about it all, especially as it was highly paid. The night before my interview the guy who was going to be my boss rang me up and had a chat to me and he sounded very nice but he said that he had done his research and knew that my experience was sketchy to say the least but to come along for the interview anyway 'as we haven't any Brits on the payroll'. He also said that if I didn't mind I'd have to take a maths test as it was compulsory for all employees. I had perfected a good telephone manner during my time at Greaterman's and told him, 'Sure, no problem!' So I turned up for the interview and sat the test. I didn't think it was particularly difficult and was finished in time to check my answers. I learnt later that it was the entrance exam for the Rand University and I had scored 100 per cent. Must have been the altitude. No, it was Scottish education. I got the job and the good pay and it was a great time for me.

The children seemed to be doing well at school and had copious loads of homework, which I checked every night. They were learning Afrikaans and Sutu as additional languages and the school was very strict. They had a nice uniform; the boys had navy blue safari suits with the school badge on the pocket and Shona had a blue and white check dress with a badge on the breast pocket. When the weather got colder the boys wore a sweater or their blazers and the girls wore pinafore skirts and jumpers. They always looked very smart. The teaching was very thorough and corporal punishment was allowed and although I never heard of them getting the cane they got plenty of slaps around the ears. I was incensed at first and wanted to go up to the school and make a fuss but I was told that if I did that they would be made fun of by the other kids so I left it. I was not to be put off, however, the day Shona came home practically falling down with fatigue and went to sleep while having her tea. The teacher had told her to stand by the fireplace for talking and had forgotten about her. She was there for hours, poor kid. I made it clear to the headmistress that I knew all about children who talked in class having dealt with them for years and I was not going to have my child treated in this way. She was very apologetic and after that there were no more complaints.

At the end of the Christmas term the school always put on a great show and the second year we were there they did a really superb version of *Alice in Wonderland*. I say it was superb, naturally, as Shona was Alice. It ran all the last week of term and was on from 7.30 p.m. till 9 p.m. As she was on stage all the time poor little Shona was exhausted and fell asleep several times when she had to sit in a chair. However, she woke up just in time to continue every night and I doubt if anyone noticed apart from the teachers and myself.

Colin had missed Shona's great stage debut as he had changed his job and was now working for the Weather Bureau. This meant that he spent a lot of time in Bethlehem, in the Orange Free State, and typically the week that Shona was doing her thing was one of those weeks. He really liked his new job though and as I was working and the children took up most of my time at home I soon got used to his being absent from Monday till Friday for six months of the year. There was a wide range of people working with him, some American and a few Afrikaaners and they had their quarters in Bethlehem in a holiday camp on Loch Athlone. Some weeks, instead of his coming home, I would pack the children and a friend or two and the two dogs into the car and drive across to spend the weekend with him. It was a very long drive of 200 miles and after working all week I was always shattered by the time I got there but it was worth it to keep the children in touch with their dad. As the company had women as well as men working there I must admit that I had a few moments of doubt about the wisdom of his being away from me for such a long period of time, but that was life and I never mentioned it. He is still here so I think my worries were normal but groundless.

I think that the way the staff at my own place of work behaved was to blame for my doubts about Colin's fidelity. There were so many office affairs going on that I lost count. I had at least three offers of company from the bosses knowing that I was a grass widow for half the year, but I'm a one man woman and couldn't be bothered so the message soon got around and there were no hard feelings. It was a very different working life to the previous two companies I had worked for and I enjoyed it tremendously. I was the only immigrant worker there but the Afrikaaners were well educated and friendly. As it was an American company there were Black and Indian people on the staff and they were great to work with. Some of them had been to university and were very clever. The Afrikaaners treated them exactly the same as they treated each other and I could see that given the chance the average South African was not in favour of the colour ban. The government imposed it on them. The offices were open plan and I had a desk next to a young Indian lad who kept me in stitches with his comments about life. One day he came in after one of the bosses had put a load of papers on his desk and he flung his hands up in the air and said, 'Would you look at my desk, it makes Soweto look tidy!'

Whenever anyone had a birthday we all met before work at the Southern Sun hotel. This was a five star hotel next to our place of work and we would have a champagne breakfast. Needless to say the company paid for it and it took a few hours of the morning to get into the work mood afterwards. There was always a stack of work and being so busy the days fairly flew past. I was trained on the computer, a big giant of a machine in its own building, and my part in it was making cards to back up my statistics and feeding them into the computer. A bit of a redundant skill nowadays, but it has helped me to understand computers and not to be afraid to tackle them. The statistic part of the job was easy and my favourite job was helping the shipping clerk. Phoning up companies who shipped our machines from America and England and generally striking up a nice friendship with our opposite numbers in those companies was the task. Unfortunately for me the shipping clerk was always there so I never got the chance to go out to dinner with the foreigners when they came over but I believe it was a sumptuous evening, all paid for by the company.

The children were growing and getting on well at school. They all had their special friends and they revelled in the sunshine. Our maid was a Zulu who was not supposed to be in the Transvaal at all but had come in desperation to try and earn some money for her family who lived near Cape Town. If we were caught employing her we would be heavily fined and she could go to prison. The police did random house visits and luckily we only had one scare. One day the boys came rushing home to tell Sara (the maid), that the police were searching the house down the road as someone had reported a maid without papers was living in the area. The maids could be quite nasty to each other and if they fell out they would phone the police and try to get each other into trouble. Well, I was at work and didn't know about this until that evening. The children hid Sara under a bed and Norman got a broom and started to clean the path in front of the house, Philip was dusting and Shona was hanging washing on the line when the police came to the house. They said, 'Is your maid in?' and Norman said, 'Would I be doing this if we had a maid?' The policeman laughed and went off. It gave us all a scare but we kept Sara and she was more like an auntie than a maid. If we rented a video she would come in and watch it with us, and as the boys always wanted cops and robbers type videos poor Sara watched with her hands over her face peeping out through her fingers. She learnt to make English food and was very fond of cooking. She could make a better shepherd's pie than I could.

Once when Colin had a week off we booked a rondavel in a holiday spot in the bush veldt called Sudwala Caves a few hours' drive away and we packed the car with kids and dogs and took off. It was raining heavily when we left home and we were all in a bit of a dejected mood by the time we got there and got to bed. In the morning we were woken by the boys and Shona who had got up early and gone exploring. The sun was out and they were so excited. Philip was saying, 'Mum, Dad this is heaven!' We got up and went outside and it did indeed look like something out of a picture book. Palm trees and a river and some minor jungle, but the most amazing thing and what had captured the boys especially was that every tree had a family of baboons hanging from it. We spent hours just watching them and they took very little notice of us. There were lovely, with little tiny babies, and one larger fiercer looking one who kept the others in line and was obviously the dominant male. It was a wonderful week. We walked and swam in the river and saw more wild birds that I couldn't even begin to identify. There were large ones and tiny little ones so highly coloured that you could hardly believe that they were real. One day we were coming back from one of our walks when a mother and father and baby giraffe walked majestically into sight. We tried to look small and stepped out of their path but they just ignored us and went on their way. I'll never forget the brightness of their colours and it made me want to cry for the poor faded giraffes in zoos all over Europe.

By now it was the South African winter and Colin was back in Pretoria and coming home every day. It was nice to have him home again. The Weather Bureau was having a new radar installed and Mr Dutoit, the boss, sent Colin to look at the tower which was being made to support it. It was being built in an Afrikaaner-staffed workshop and the boss said, 'Well man, what do you want?', not at all welcoming. Colin produced the plans and pointed out that the tower was supposed to be ten feet tall and they had made it five feet. Well, there were a few red faces around that workshop.

Soon it was time for us to go home for our promised trip. We had been in South Africa two and a half years by then and although I cannot say that I missed the UK I was a bit anxious to see the family again. We were in fairly constant contact with them but they seemed so far away. Colin's father had died and Colin didn't even know about it until a week after the funeral. So off we went, by plane this time and we had a good time. My brothers met us at the airport and it was great to see them. They had all got older looking especially Donald John whose hair was pure white. The other two boys had a good 50 per cent of white sprinkled among the brown but as I had dyed my hair blonde a few years before as I could see the white coming in I had no room to talk. We had worked out that the best way for us to see all the family was to travel by train, spending a few days in London, then on to Bristol, back to Glasgow to see Alick my youngest brother, on to the Hebrides and back to Bristol to say our farewells and on to London and the plane back to South Africa. We had left the dogs behind with Sara who was keeping the house safe while we were away.

It was lovely to see all the MacMillans in London: Donald Angus and Sheila with their children Catherine and Gordon; Donald John and Brenda with their two daughters Kay and Suzanne and young Martin; Mary Flora and Ian and their three girls, Elaine, Gillian and Emma; and Donald and Peggy with their two daughters, Karen and Tracey. As I've explained before, all the Donald names in our family was because of the common Hebridean way of naming your sons after family members and our family had Donalds on both sides to be remembered so we always used the second name as well to avoid any mix ups. We have always been a very close family although I lived far away from them for most of my life starting with being farmed out to my aunties in Benbecula and then on to Barra. It made them all very dear to me and being with them all again was a joy. We stayed at Donald John's house and the others came to visit. A grand party was had with Brenda's brother, Wyndham, and his wife coming up from Eweshot and the garage was decked out with decorations and a record player so that all the children could have their own party. Great stuff.

Soon we were loaded on to the train to go to Bristol. We had a nice journey but as we had been too busy talking and partying the previous day we hadn't realized that the Queen and the Royal family were visiting Bristol that day. When we got to Temple Meads station it was cordoned off for the Royal train and the public had to stay outside the station. That is all the public except Colin's brother Ken. He had somehow managed to get in and was standing in solitary splendour on the platform. Good man.

The Bristol trip was great and it was lovely to see them all again. They were exclaiming over our tans and the boys' blonde hair and we were amazed at how their children had become so grown up in two years. Colin's mother was getting on and her sight was failing but she had hired a hall and got all the relatives organized for a party. I think our children must have thought that we were very important people to have such a fuss made of us and they really enjoyed it all. Soon it was time to board the train and make for the north. Alick met us in Glasgow and we had a lovely evening with him and his friends at the local pub. One of his friends babysat for us and the children were really amazed at the wealth of TV programmes available to the UK people as our TV programmes were mostly in Afrikaans and the English ones only good for a laugh as the quality was terrible.

We had arranged to fly from Glasgow to Benbecula as it saved a bit of time and also we were all feeling tired after all the travelling. My father met us at Benbecula and although I was delighted to see him I was struck by the way he had aged so much in a short time. Well, I found out from my mother that he had been drinking again and he was very disappointed that none of the family wanted to come and take over the croft that he had held in good order over the years. It was a visit which I try to forget as I felt that we were partly to blame for his morose behaviour. My mother was her usual cheerful self but I kept thinking that she didn't have much of a life. The aunties were getting on in age but glad to see us and we visited them several times. Each time the table groaned with every delicacy you could think of. They tried to tell me all about dad's misdeeds while we were away but with the children taking up much of their attention, mercifully, I managed to keep the peace. I won't deny that I was glad to get away. The day before we left I was having a tear or two in the bedroom and Colin came in with a plan. 'Why don't you stay here with the children and help them out. I'll go back alone and finish the contract and then come back.' I won't tell you my answer to that, except that Colin left the bedroom very quickly and never mentioned that plan again. The way I saw it I was a very minor part of the family and to give up the life I had worked hard for at that stage was just not on, not for me or for my family. Come the time when the croft would be passed on I had no illusions about my rights. I had none. And time has proved me right. My parents are both gone now and I own not a blade of my father's grass. I am fine about it as we have all we will ever need, bought and paid for by our own efforts, and that is good enough for me.

So with a sigh of relief we boarded the plane and took off for England again. Colin's family had booked us in to a holiday camp on Hayling Island, a place we had been to before and as it was the British summer we had a lovely time. Colin's mother was there and Ken, Beryl and all their family so we had two chalets, next door to each other. The sun shone every day and we sunbathed by day and played cards at night. A great time was made even greater by an unexpected phone call from Canada. One of Peggy's sons had got a cheap flight for her and she was coming over for a week. Well, that was very exciting but the camp was full and our chalets were already bursting at the seams. The camp manager came to our rescue and said that he would clear out the tiny hut where the deck chairs were kept and put a bed in there for her and that was fine. We had a ball! It was a great time for Colin's mother having all her family together around her and for us it was the icing on the cake.

As the boys were growing up and would soon be required to take out a South African passport, and go to the border for their National Service in a few years time, we had no illusions about staying in South Africa long term. So we made tentative enquiries about the possibility of coming back and settling in Bristol. This was given a good reception and Ken and Beryl told us that we could rely on them to give us any help we needed when the time came. So, much heartened, we said our farewells and set off back to the airport. We saw the MacMillans again in London and I expressed my fears about the situation back home, but they said that there was little they could do, living so far away. Donald John was getting on very well in Special Branch CID and was the prime minister's bodyguard, spending a lot of time in Buckingham Palace and all over the place. The other two boys and Mary Flora were busy with their jobs and families and couldn't really do anything either. So I blocked it out of my head and got on with my own life.

It was getting toward the end of the winter season when we got back to South Africa and although the mornings were frosty your steering wheel would burn your hands by lunch time. Strange climate but you got used to it. Our friends, Derek and Betty, gave us a great welcome back and we had an evening of holiday tales at our house where we played the Billy Connolly LP which was his first, and we all laughed till the tears ran down our faces. We had never heard such an irreverent comedian, but that was long ago.

Back at work the old computer was being scrapped and some new ones were being installed. This meant a lot of work for me as my statistics now had to be transferred to the new machine, which was a complete mystery to me as well as to the bosses. Their attitude was 'You're from the UK, Chris, this machine was made in the UK so what's your problem?' Well I got on with it, and the handbook and I spent many nights together. It was a good job that Colin was once again in the Free State as I would have had little time to talk to him.

Norman had reached the top class in primary school and was transferring to secondary school in Kempton Park. A much rougher environment than his primary school, but as many of his classmates were going with him we just let him go with them. I would have liked to have seen him go to one of the private schools as we could have afforded the fees but I was outvoted and that was that. In hindsight when we returned to the UK it would have been an expense we could well do without so maybe it was for the best. The school was pretty rough but he never complained, not even the day he came home after being held down and imprisoned in a coffin made of rocks. He had a good go at the culprits on the way home from school and was a mess when I saw him. Bloody nose, black eye etc. One of his assailants lived round the corner from us so I decided to walk over and have a go at him, until I went into the house and saw him. If anything he had more cuts and bruises than Norman and his mother and I decided to keep out of it. As it happened they both went off to school together the next day and the fight seemed to be forgotten.

Christmas that year is one that I remember as Norman got an air rifle, which he had wanted for ages. Colin showed him how to use it and set up a target on the garage wall for him and his friends to practice on. Things were going fine until one day I noticed that the streetlight outside our house was off. The municipality replaced the bulb but it went off again two days later and this went on for weeks. Finally I rang them up and complained bitterly. 'Mrs Hall do you know that as soon as we repair the light, your son shoots it with his air rifle.' Well, was my face red? Norman's air rifle was confiscated and sold. Hindsight tells me that he was too young to have it in the first place and I can thank God that it wasn't a more serious misdemeanour.

The last week of term at the primary school was always spent at the Kruger National Park by the departing top class. Norman went and came back with some great photos. However, the following year, it was Philip's turn and by some rotten coincidence the teacher who was taking them was one with whom he had had a long running feud throughout the whole of his primary schooling. She was a geography teacher and was pretty hopeless. Often she would state things which were wrong and Phil, being an avid reader with a photographic memory, would correct her and prove her wrong. Well, she got her own back – she refused to take him. I went up to the school and pleaded with the Head but there was nothing she could do. She said that she understood the problem but it was out of her hands as she let the geography department take care of all the arrangements for that year. She had tears in her eyes when I told her that Philip had been waiting for his turn to go to the

Kruger with the school ever since we got to South Africa, and now we would be leaving soon and he would never get the chance again. Well, there was no change, the teacher was adamant and Philip probably learnt a lesson at great cost. His long term friend Robin Marsden had also been dying to go and had been accepted, but when he heard that Philip had been excluded he said, 'Well they can go without me as well.' I think that was a great show of friendship. Colin took both the boys to Bethlehem with him for a week and saw to it that they had a great time, but I'm sure that Philip still thinks of that as one of the saddest times in his young life.

Shona was a few years behind the boys in school and as they frequently told her that she was just a 'stupid girl' she believed them. She was in Brownies and dance class and she and her friend, Melanie, had a very full life. I remember coming home early from work one day and meeting her on the road. She was on her way to drama club, wearing her Brownie uniform for the next event and on the handlebars of her bike were her ballet pumps for the final class of the day. 'I can't stop, Mum, I'm late,' she shouted to me as she whizzed past. When she was out of the Infant's section she got her first report card and it was very good. I'll never forget her face when she presented me with it, 'I have got a brain mum, the boys were wrong!' she said.

Chapter Nine

AFTER OUR BRITISH HOLIDAY WE knew that coming back was inevitable. We either came back and lived in Bristol or the other alternative was to go to Canada. One of my friends at my previous place of work had done this and we got rave letters from her about how nice it was etc., and of course Peggy, Colin's sister, lived there and would be very happy to have us in the same country. However, when we investigated the possibility we found that we would be bound by the sanctions against South Africa which were now in place and it meant that we would have to go back to England, then apply for entry to Canada, and pay our own fares. As we were going to have to pay our fares to get back to the UK we thought that we'd put an end to our travels and stay there. Although the nasty depression was still gripping the UK we thought we'd take our chance, after all we had made a tidy bit of money in South Arica which would see us through.

Well, that was a good idea . . . not! On further investigation we found that we could only take out of

South Africa the money we had brought in, and the rand had plummeted in value so we could actually take about three quarters of our original stock of money, made by selling our house before we left. At that moment we were thankful that the depression had brought house prices down in England and that as well as the money to buy a house, at least we had enough rands to pay for a good passage and have the dogs transported and kenneled for the six months period required by the quarantine laws. This was not included in the actual money transfer but, thank goodness, we had been a bit careful about our spending as we could easily have gone into the wild spending sprees we had seen some of our friends engaging in. As Norman would have to go into a secondary school we asked him if he would mind going back three months before us to start his education at the beginning of the school term and he was delighted and excited to be going to Bristol to stay at Uncle Ken's on his own. He was allowed to take a certain amount of money with him as an independent traveller and that also helped. So with our plans made for the future we settled down to life in the land that was entering its death throes as heaven for the whites and nobody else. Colin would finish his contract with his employer then we would sell the house and off we would go.

Most of our friends tried to talk us out of our decision to leave. Our immigrant friends were saying, 'Stay, it will be a good few years before you need to go.' But we didn't want our boys going to the border to fight a war we did not believe in and although we loved the country, the people and the lifestyle, our minds were made up. We were determined that we would not leave a cent of our hard earned cash behind and so we had a very good last year in South Africa.

We took numerous holidays, some on our own and some with Betty, Derek and their two girls. We used to go to a place called Utopia, which was just like heaven. The terrain was similar to that which we had found at Sudwala Caves but it was a much bigger development. Rondavels to sleep in – huts made of tree logs and roofed with grass, containing the usual sleeping, dining and seating areas – and if they were a bit primitive they were a perfect antidote to the lavish style that we town folk were used to. We all had a great relaxing time there. Walking, swimming, and just talking for hours on end, we would put South Africa to rights then start on the rest of the world. There were never many people there and the rondavels were well spaced so that you could go for a week without seeing anyone else.

Some things stick in the mind and I can still see this scene quite clearly: the day we were out walking and there across the path was a giant of a snake. It was a good eight feet long and nearly a foot wide. I have never seen one so big, except in a zoo. After the usual squeals and squeaks of horror we approached it and poked it with sticks to find that it was dead. Well, Colin had his camera and took a few photos and Philip asked him to take a special photo so that he could show his friends back at school. He picked the snake up, with difficulty as it was pretty heavy, so we all had to lend a hand, and hold it above his head. 'Hurry up, Dad!' he called and the snake's stomach which was just above his head burst. I'll never forget the smell and I don't think poor Philip will either. He was absolutely covered in the most awful slimy mess of snake food digested and half eaten . . . aw, it was vile. Unfortunately Colin had dropped the camera when the wave of stench hit him but I'm sure we can all recall the incident clearly.

Snakes were always a part of our lives in South Africa, especially with Norman and Philip about. They had no fear of them whatsoever and they and their school friends would go out in the veldt and search for them after school. If they found a boomslang (a South African spitting cobra), they would put goggles on and one would poke it with a a stick until it reared up, put its hood up and spat venom at one of them while the other took a photo. Fortunately I learnt about this after I came back from South Africa and saw the photos or they would have been tied to the table for the duration.

On one occasion I was driving them back from the Free State after a visit to their dad and reached out to move a box of matches that was on the dashboard. 'Don't touch that box, Mum. It's full of scorpions!' said Norman. Well, I stopped the car, the matchbox went out of the window and the boys were threatened with having to walk home if they ever did that again

When we were packing up some of our stuff before selling the house I used to pack some boxes during the week and store them in the garage and Colin would carry on the task when he came home at the weekend. One Saturday I heard some shouting coming from the garage and it was Colin. He had opened a box and there was a spitting cobra rising up to attack him. He hastily tied the box up and called the boys. Sure enough they had captured the snake and owned up to another box full of numerous other snakes that they were going to take to school. Colin made them take both boxes out on to the veldt and release the snakes with threats of all sorts of grisly punishments if they ever went near another snake or anything venomous.

Of course the boat had to be sold before we left and that caused a lot of grief especially to Colin and Norman who just lived for the sailing club, but it had to be. So, with heavy hearts, they advertised it at the club and it went very quickly. I must admit that I felt quite tearful as they had had so much fun with it and it was a large part of our lives. Colin said that we'd get another one, even better, and sail it on the many dams and sailing clubs in Bristol but, like many other things, the new boat never materialized, life was different for all of us when we made the move.

I told the people at work that we were leaving and had the usual, 'You'll change your mind.' And, 'You'll be back in six months, when the cold and the depression hits you, we'll keep your job for you.' They simply couldn't believe that we were actually going to leave what they thought of as the promised land and go back to England. However, we could see the signs of South Africa being totally isolated by the other countries and didn't want our children's futures to be jeopardized. So, Britain was in the grips of a depression but that couldn't last and we were definitely going. We started selling off our furniture and all the other bits and bobs which we didn't want to take back with us and got a very good price for everything, mostly from the black and coloured staff at work. I remember a nice black man who worked in the stores department buying our electric lawn mower. He told me the next day that he'd mowed all the grass round his house and the children in the village were all watching him. 'When it started to rain they all shouted, "The electric will kill you." So I went in and put on some rubber gloves,' he said. We also had a lot of kitchen stuff that we had bought and the managing director's private secretary who was Zulu expressed an interest, so I asked her to come and have a look one Saturday. We waited and waited for a long time but she didn't turn up so we went out. When we came back she was sleeping in the grass by our gate. This was a girl who could put any of us to shame in the office and was always beautifully dressed. There was definitely a difference between the South African natives and our immigrant black population in the UK – probably arrested development caused by their dreadful living conditions, but that was not their fault.

And so the last year shot by and Philip started secondary school at Boksburg High, as we knew that we would have to rent a house in that area for our final few months before leaving. We sold our lovely house in Bonaero Park and moved and Norman packed and left. It was a strange time for all of us. We didn't want to go at all but knew that we had been lucky to have lived in a South Africa which was fast disappearing, and to get away while we still could. As the dogs had to be in quarantine for six months back in UK we made the arrangements and sent them off back to a kennel in the Forest of Dean, so that part of their quarantine would be over before we got back and got our house. Some people just left their dogs behind and every day the poor dogs would turn up at the school gates waiting for the children to come out of school. Their old friends, the children, were back home in the UK or Germany or wherever and the dog wagon would come to the school, pick them up and take them to the abattoir be put down. It used to break my heart. We didn't even consider the possibility of giving our dogs to the many people who expressed an interest in them. Where we went, no matter the expense, so would they go.

So it was a strange quiet house in Impala Park, no Norman and no dogs and precious little furniture. A week after we had moved the children's bikes were stolen. A policeman came to the house and took the details and surprise, surprise the bikes were found. Now I had seen a couple of little black boys lurking about a few days before the bikes vanished and as we were near the reservation where they lived, I thought that they'd got lost and spoke to them but they ran away. I mentioned this to the policeman and he took a note of it. A few days later I was asked to go to the police station at Kempton Park as they had two boys that they suspected of being the culprits and wanted me to identify them. The day came and I presented myself full of righteous indignation about my children's bikes being stolen. While I waited for my turn I saw a large Afrikaaner policeman walking away down a corridor holding a little back boy by the hand and in his other hand was a whip. Now I don't know what the story behind that was or what the ending of the story was but my imagination did the business. When the two little boys who had been near our house were brought out for me to identify them I swore blind that I had never seen them before in my life. I even said that the ones I had seen were much bigger. I could see the little boys' eyes widen in surprise and I waited until they were released and ran for their lives out of the police station. I knew it was them, they knew that I knew, and from his angry expression the policeman who questioned me also knew that I knew, but at least I could sleep that night.

Although the dogs had gone we were soon taken over by another animal. A little kitten had entered our lives and refused to be frightened off. I suspect the children helped her to become one of us. She was terrible to live with and Shona called her Mataevus which I think was Afrikaans for mischievous. She must have been the daughter of a wild cat as she was not like any cat I've ever known. Completely clean in the house, thank goodness, but she had some strange ways. When she wanted to go out or come in she would not mew or sit at the door, she would jump up on your back and hiss. Then while you picked up the cup you had just dropped she would run to the door and scratch some more paint off. If she wanted a drink she would ignore the saucer of milk always left out for her and instead jump up to the sink and attack the taps. Cups, saucers, anything left on the draining boards went flying. The spare bedroom was full of boxes in which we were packing the rest of the children's toys and books and the usual last minute stuff. Mataevus was a very good hunter and would bring home small birds and mice and bury them in the boxes among the toys and books, tearing up the newspapers and packing materials. So each time you went to pack anything you had to first of all empty the box and bury all the dead stuff she had packed. A few days later you would find a big hole in the garden and all the dead creatures piled up on the front doorstep. One thing we did not have to be afraid of was stray dogs or cats coming into our garden as Mataevus would creep up behind any animal and jump on its back, clawing and hissing till it ran for its life. Unfortunately the postman also came into the unwanted category so after a few attempts he just put the letters on the gatepost and ran away.

One day the house was very quiet, there were no crashing noises in the kitchen and no dead animals on the step or in the boxes, and no Mataevus. We told the children that she must have moved on to another family, but still they kept calling her and looking for her without success. The children even went out on to the veldt and called for her but there was no sign. One day about a week after she had gone Colin was tidying up outside and he remembered that the coal bunker still had a few loads of coal in it, enough to make some fires for our neighbour, so he asked Philip to give him a hand and empty it. It was an old fashioned concrete box-like structure with a flap on the top and a slit at the bottom where you could put your shovel in to get the coal. Well, when they looked at the slit there was a little black hairy paw sticking out of it. Mataevus. They opened the flap and there she was, very hungry, very weak, hissing a little and very angry. There was great rejoicing and once she had been cleaned and fed and kissed by the children they came to the conclusion that although they had played with her and fed her before we had all been too busy to acknowledge that poor Mataevus had no voice. So we bought a bell, which she wore round her neck and made sure that we always knew where she was. The bell put an end to her creature catching, but she had plenty of food anyway. We knew that she needed a special home when we left for the UK and we found one with a woman who loved her story and lived alone in a large house. Mataevus was going to have her own bedroom and bathroom . . . well.

And so the magic time in South Africa came to an end. We were all packed and the handover of my job at work was being arranged. I thought that we would have the usual farewell drink at the Southern Sun before work on my last day and a wave as I left but I was wrong. When I left work the previous day I asked if we were all meeting up at the hotel in the morning and my boss said, 'No, why?' I thought, 'Well, well, so they're going to let me go without even a farewell drink.' But not so. When I arrived at work the next day the rest of the staff were all there, and I mean all the staff. The computer floor of the building was packed and all the desks had been put to one side and covered with tablecloths loaded with every kind of delicacy. One table had a notice on it, 'Things You are Going To Miss', and that table had all the South African dishes that I had expressed interest in and had badgered people until they got the recipes for me. Among the food there were photos of people I had been especially friendly with, my shady car-parking spot that I had battled for, my last payslip and all sorts of funny things. There was no work done in the building that day. It was eating and drinking and so many speeches that I couldn't count them – they even got the people from Germany, America and England with whom I had dealt when doing shipping to send messages on the computer wishing me well. I was absolutely flabbergasted and watched my drinking carefully as I had to drive home. As I left the building for the last time with shouts of, 'If you come back come to us first if you want a job' ringing in my ears, I thought how much I would have liked to have grown old there had things been different.

Colin had his farewell parties at work and one evening meal his boss put on was quite memorable: we got so lost on the way to his house that we were two hours late. We rang him up from a call box to get directions and Colin said, 'We are so late that we couldn't possibly come now.' But his boss said that his wife had kept the dinner hot and to come anyway. Well we finally found the house and were given a great if slightly fuzzy welcome as obviously Pete Dutoit and his wife had been having the odd drink to pass the time. I'll always remember the martinis he kept mixing for me. I had asked for a martini, meaning the ready-mixed one which came in a bottle and was not very strong, but Pete mixed his own with gin and vermouth and bitters and goodness knows what else, each one stronger than the last. By the time I was on my third I did not know whether it was six o'clock or

Christmas day. We staggered out to the car and got lost again on the way home. Finally, the car had had enough and the engine died on a piece of isolated veldt in the early hours of the morning. I was content to curl up and go to sleep but Colin made me get out and walk back with him to a house he had noticed us passing. We got to the house eventually and woke up the Afrikaans farmer who lived there. To give him his due he was sympathetic and gave us a lift home in his stinking cattle truck. The next day Colin collected the car and took it to the garage to be repaired. It was already sold so the bill was not very welcome.

To be truthful I didn't feel bad about leaving the house in Impala Park for the last time. I'd shed all my tears when leaving our lovely home with the swimming pool, probably knowing that that would be our last taste of such opulence. The children were both excited about going back to England and seeing their relatives and Norman, and they talked about snow and things we never saw in South Africa, so that helped. Our flight to England was leaving early in the morning so we stayed overnight at the airport hotel and had a great farewell with Betty and Derek and their family and our Afrikaans friends, Sid and Ann and their family. It felt unreal and I was really regretting having to leave them. They were still trying to change our minds and I remember saying to Betty, 'If you had two boys instead of your girls you'd be doing the same.' However, we said our last farewells and despite corresponding with them all over the years, we haven't seen them since. We did keep in touch with Betty's mother for a while after we came back as Betty wasn't answering my letters. We were stunned to hear that Betty and Derek had parted and were getting a divorce. They had both been having affairs but despite seeing them every week for three years we hadn't even noticed. How dumb can you be?

The flight from Johannesburg and the rest of the journey was uneventful and we met the MacMillans at London airport. As we were flying down to Bristol it was a quick coffee and off. We knew that we'd be seeing plenty of them in the future. At the airport in Bristol we were met by all the close family members of the Hall clan and driven to Ken's house. There was also a tall young man with a crew cut with them and I had difficulty recognising Norman who had grown at least six inches and whose floppy blonde haircut was now a memory. The Bristol boys were all wearing short hair and so he had followed suit. The lack of sun to bleach his hair resulted in it going back to brown, as it has been ever since.

It was lovely to be back and although we were a bit of a crowd for Beryl to accommodate we were sure that we could soon be in our own home and established. Well, it took us six weeks and eventually we were back on track albeit on the bottom of the housing ladder once again. Colin had to get a job, any old job would do to allow us to get a mortgage, and we settled down to Bristol life in a very small semi-detached house near Ken and Beryl's. When I say small I mean minute. When we were all sitting down in the lounge and one of us wanted to go out of the room the others had to stand up, that small! However we were glad to be on our own again and were optimistic.

The children had started school and the boys seemed to be getting along fine but poor Shona was not too happy. The children in her class were a sadistic lot who used to say things like, 'You're from Africa, you must be black under the skin.' And they would scratch her arms to see if this was the case. Her work was streets ahead of the children in her class so this didn't help. She had been taught the cursive style of writing in South Africa and this was not permissible in Bristol so she had to try and write in a different fashion. Her writing has never recovered. When I heard that she was being bullied I went up to the school but the Head told me that there was little he could do; she just had to 'tough it out' he said. Shona herself was horrified that I had gone to the school and made me swear on the Bible that I would never again do that. One day however she came home with a note asking me to go and see the Head and despite me asking what it was about she wouldn't say what the problem was. So I went up there with my heart in my mouth.

Well, when I got to the school I was surprised to be greeted very warmly by the secretary who ushered me into the Head's office. 'Don't worry, Mrs Hall,' he said, 'We are not going to punish Shona and we just called you in so that the boy's parents will think we are giving you a lecture.' I was completely mystified. Then he told me that the boy in class who sat behind Shona had been at the root of all the nastiness she had undergone. The previous day a new girl had started and he had a new person to taunt and terrify. This new girl was sitting beside Shona and the boy was dipping her plaits into his inkwell, putting stuff down her back, poking her with his pencil and generally making her life a misery. Shona stood it for a short while and then turned around and gave him a huge uppercut right on the jaw. He was howling with pain and they had to send him to hospital in an ambulance as she had nearly broken his jaw. 'You'd never think a fragile little thing like Shona could do that,' the Head said. 'All the teachers have been dying to do it for years.' Well, that was the end of the bullying period and

I'm happy to say that she was quite happy in school after that. At first she missed Melanie, her South African friend, sorely, but time heals all wounds and new friends take the place of old ones.

At this point I will leave my children out of my tale as they deserve to live their lives and write about it themselves when they get to my age. I would not have thanked my mother or father for writing about me. We are all good friends and I would like us to remain so, apart from an occasional mention which will no doubt slip out, that is it.

We had a very quick exit from the tiny house. As soon as Colin had got a reasonable job and I was working at a local office we moved to a large semi-detached house where we could all fit in and leave the room without needing a family manoeuvre. I got tired of office work and went back to teaching as the pay was much better. I got to know people and places in Bristol, which had become a different city to the one I knew when I first visited it. The immigrant population had spread out of the city centre and the lovely block of flats where Colin's mother used to live had become a ghetto. At least that's what I thought. Drugs and other problems had become prolific and there were beggars on most of the inner city streets. Fortunately we lived on the outskirts of the city and it was a relatively civilized spot. However, my school where I taught the Special Needs class was in one of the poorer areas, Knowle West, and it was like another country. To make matters worse the headmaster was very strange. On one parents evening, he came into my room where I was talking to the last parent, a man who had just come out of prison for assaulting another with a deadly weapon and who reeked of booze. I was glad to see the Head coming in, thinking that he was making sure that I had support. Not likely, he threw the school keys on my desk and said, 'You're the only one left in the building, Chris, lock up when you leave. I'm off.' I wrapped up that interview very quickly and shot off home. I was frightened. The children in my class were all from very poor homes and they had no real interest in learning, but, as with most children in the poorer areas, they were full of life and I decided to make Special Needs my subject for the rest of my teaching days. I did a course in the various strategies to test and maximize the children's abilities and really enjoyed the work. It is amazing the number of pupils who, once they learned to read, caught up with their age group. The pride that they took in being able to exhibit their work was wonderful. God bless them.

Chapter Ten

ONE OF THE GREATEST ADVANTAGES of being back once again in the United Kingdom was the ease with which we could contact both sides of the family. Even the Uist contingent were only a few hours away by train or plane and so we were in constant touch. My father, after being a strong active man all his life, had developed an ailment that seemed to puzzle the doctors and they tried various tablets and combinations of medicines to help him. He responded quite well, but was suffering a dreadful memory loss, which was worrying. He had always been so fit and such a hard worker that it worried us all. To look at, he was fine, but just now and again he'd say or do something completely out of place and you would realize that all was far from well. His drinking days were well and truly over and he and my mother lived a quiet life up in South Uist. She, having had plenty of nursing experience, knew just how to deal with him but, unfortunately, the years of living in a damp climate and all the outside work she had done meant that her own health was far from good and her legs were always giving her a lot of pain.

When we visited there was always an air of festivity and the past was given a good going over. They had a chest of drawers in one of the bedrooms full of photographs. Some had been put in albums but my favourite drawer was the one full of loose photos from the distant past. My father would say, '*Tha i a'tighinn le luma lan na draghair de dhaoine marbh.*' (Here she comes with a drawerful of dead people.) So they were, some of them, but I knew that they had meant something to either himself or my mother for the photos to be in there. And that is how and when I got to know my Benbecula uncles. There had been a very large family of them. Alan, the eldest, I knew as he lived in Benbecula on the old croft, but there was John, Donald John, Peter, Donald, and Angus whom I either had never met or it was at a time when I was too young to have had two words with them. I vaguely remembered seeing Donald John and another one during the war in RAF uniforms. Angus, also, had spent a few days in Kilpheder with his wife when he had got married, but I had never seen John, Peter or Donald. Donald had died young and all the rest of them were living somewhere on the mainland. They must have gone home to visit their parents at some time but I can't remember seeing them in Kilpheder. All my father's tales seemed to be about people from South Uist and there was very little about his childhood or his brothers. Strange that.

I have recently been given several photos by one of my young cousins, and will endeavour to include them in case there is anybody out there who remembers the MacMillan boys from Sliabh na h-Airde, Benbecula. There was one girl, Mary Margaret, and I spent many an afternoon at her house in Glasgow when I was a student at Notre Dame College. She, her husband and two children, Flora and Roddie, all died years ago and were much missed. She always spent some time at our house as did her children whenever she visited Benbecula and in later years she moved to Garrynamonie to the small croft house in which her husband's people had lived. But that was after I had left the island. I suppose that in this day of looking up your family tree on the computer it would be easy enough for me to find out everything about them but somehow I never seem to take that track. Maybe one day.

Showing my father the old photos was never very fruitful: he'd say, 'That's Peter, or that's Alan', but very little else. At the time I didn't notice but now I find it strange that someone who was so voluble on everything in his life since marriage and moving to South Uist had so little to say about his own family or childhood in Benbecula. I was with him when he got the news of his mother's death. He was down on the croft haymaking and I was in the house, doing my Daliburgh School homework. My mother came home from the Daliburgh shops and said, 'Will you please go and tell your father that his mother has died.' I went down and told him, '*Dh'eug Grannie Mhor.*' (Big Granny has died.) He went down on one knee and said a prayer. His hands were over his eyes but I could see the tears streaming down his face from behind them. Then he got up and carried on with the haymaking. I stood by but my heart broke for my poor dad. They both went down to Benbecula for the funeral a few days later. I can't remember my grandfather at all so he must have died when I was very little, although one of the photos my cousin gave me has me sitting on Granny Mhor's lap beside a man who must have been my grandfather. As I was wearing a fluffy hat and rompers I must have only been a few months old so my lack of recall is forgivable.

Sometimes my mother and father would visit us in Bristol and it was lovely to be able to take them out and do things with them. My mother loved shopping but dad's erratic behaviour made it impossible for us to take him with us and we had to concoct some story to make him stay behind with Colin. He didn't like it one bit and would sulk like mad when we got home. Colin's mother got on really well with him and although she was a good few years older and losing her sight they would sit together and talk and laugh for ages. When she left he'd say, 'She is a real lady that one.' And then my mother would be the one with the sulks.

We had a real scare some years before when my young brother Alick had a brain hemorrhage. He made a good recovery and although it left him with epilepsy and eventually he was unable to keep on working, his medication took care of it and he filled his days quite happily writing and painting. The rest of the family seemed to be in good health so it was a dreadful blow when Donald John was taken to hospital with stomach pains and diagnosed with advanced cancer. It was pretty much incurable and a few months later he was gone. My childhood friend. My protector at Fort William school. My brother whom the whole family looked up to. The one who kept in touch with me wherever in the world I happened to be. A poet and a man who had no enemies. With a brilliant life in Special Branch CID and a good future ahead of him, he never saw fifty. How could I envisage a world without him? Deep darkness in my heart. The world didn't matter now. I know that the rest of the family thought me hardhearted for not going up to London to be with him for his last few days in the hospital, but I could not face the fact that he was dying and I could not face him. So I tried to get on with my life in Bristol until I got the phone call to say that he had gone. I remember my amazement at the fact that the man next door was cutting his grass and that birds were singing outside in the garden. How could all this be going on when Donald John was dead?

We all went to the funeral which was absolutely packed with people from Uist, London, Lewis and all over. There were a great many from Scotland Yard and Detective Chief Superintendent Ison gave the eulogy. I don't remember it all but here are bits of it:

> It is said that the good die young and in no case is this more apposite than in the case of Donald MacMillan.
>
> He was a man known to all of you, the husband, the son, the father, the brother, the friend, the musician, the songwriter, the colleague, the policeman, yet to all of us he is the same man.
>
> He was the epitome of gentleness and courtesy, the quiet unassuming Hebridean Scot, a man whose manner would turn away wrath.
>
> 'To have walked with kings' is in many cases a trite phase but in Don's case it was true, he did walk with kings and with prime ministers and by each he was admired and respected. An attribute sought by many, achieved by few, but achieved by Don with so little effort.
>
> As a policeman he was the model of all we seek to emulate, in life as well as in our profession . . . a pourer of oil on troubled waters, full of sound Gaelic wisdom with an underlying humour . . . and always a readiness to make fun of himself.

He was the ideal shadow for a prime minister, behaving professionally as he did privately. Always there but never obtrusive . . .

We come here today with heavy hearts, because we did not want to lose him. He was a man of whom it can justly be said – and of most men it can so rarely be said – he had no enemies.

He was a man the world could ill afford to lose.

I remember my pride when listening to Ison's words and thinking, not bad for the little boy who slept four to a bed in a thatched cottage with no running water and attended Daliburgh School. He did it all himself. Well, life goes on as they say, but since that day it has never been the same for me.

My parents were very brave and my mother showed the courage with which she had faced all the frustrations and heartbreak that life had thrown in her path. She was never seen to cry and when I asked her how she managed she said, 'I go to the bathroom and lock the door and let the tears come, then it doesn't upset your father.' My own way was a bit similar. I used to wait until Colin and the children were asleep and then I'd get up and go downstairs and give in to my terrible grief. One night I was huddled on the settee crying and I heard Donald John's voice in my head, 'Stop it now, Chrissie, I am very tired and I have to go.' The tears dried on my face and I went to bed. That was the last time I indulged in tears for him, until now. As I write about that terrible time I can't help it. It was many years ago but I am still sure that Donald John's spirit was with me in that room at that moment and that one day we will all be together. My father had been in hospital several times and Donald John had made the effort to go up and visit him more than any of us. And he always took a dark suit and a black tie with him, in case my father died. Well, my father was the one who wore mourning for him. It's a strange world.

Life in Bristol had become a bit bizarre. I was teaching and getting on very well in my job; having left the first school with its strange headmaster I was running the Special Needs department at a local school and coaching the netball team in my spare time. Colin had joined SERCO and had been sent to Benbecula! So he was in my homeland and I was in his. He came home every six weeks and pleaded with us to uproot and move to Uist, but the children were settled in their schools and I was not in favour of yet another move at that time. So we went on living our separate lives for a while. It wasn't easy with three teenagers and a full time job but I was so busy with it all that the time fairly flew. I made a few trips up to Uist but eventually Colin got a transfer to the Motorways Department and came back to Bristol. So it all worked out well. Shona had rekindled her interest in drama and was doing well with the Bristol drama club so we went to see her plays and eisteddfods regularly.

Now that things were getting better in the finance department and we could afford to be a bit more adventurous with our holidays we started going over to Canada to visit Colin's sister Peggy and her family who lived near Niagara Falls just over the American border. At last I got to see the place I was due to emigrate to when I met Colin. It was everything I dreamt of in those far off days. Whether I would have had a better life if I had gone there in my early twenties or not I shall never know, but I have been well content with my life as it turned out. Peggy and the family always made our visits a gala occasion and we were taken all over the place to see the country and generally have a good time. Shona went with us the first two times we went there and she enjoyed it as much as we did. We went over the border to visit Peggy's daughter, Beverly, who lives in Glens Falls in New York State and were always given the gala treatment there. We also visited cousins of theirs, Pat and Jim McSherry, in Ottowa and were taken to their summer-house out on the lakes – a marvellous experience. Jim had a speedboat and he spent an entire afternoon teaching Shona to water-ski. Her bottom must have hit the water a thousand times.

One visit to Canada which I will always remember was the time Peggy decided to take us to a Native American village to see a pageant. We went off in the early evening and after a few wrong turnings and trying to follow the hopelessly muddled directions found our selves pretty much lost. Fortunately we came across a petrol station and the owners pointed us in the right direction. They did, however, express their concerns about us going out there after dark as someone had been murdered on that road a few nights before. Having come so far we decided to give it a go and it all seemed pretty quiet until we got to the village, which was in festive mood. We did notice that we were the only white people there but the Native Americans all looked OK and we wandered around looking at the stalls and buying the odd souvenir at grossly high prices until it was time to go to the auditorium for the show. The setting looked idyllic. It was out of doors, around a small lake with an island in the middle. Wooden seats surrounded the lake and as they were on a hill it looked just like an outdoor theatre so we sat down. That was when the evening started to go wrong. The seats were on a slope and you had to dig your feet into the ground to stay on them.

Then the play began and it was an old Indian legend

which, if done by professionals might have been fine, but it was so badly done it was torture. They had a taped storyline and the actors kept falling out of sequence with it. 'And out of the hills in the evening mist came the brave with his gift for the Chief' ... the little boat would have arrived before the storyline was played and a young native American in jeans and a Grateful Dead T-shirt passed a Kentucky Fried Chicken box to a guy in the big headdress. Honestly, I am the most forgiving of people when it comes to amateur productions as I have done them and produced them, but this was so bad, and the audience was lapping it up. I caught Peggy's eye and she was choking with laughter. Her son who was sitting beside her, whispered fiercely, 'For God's sake don't laugh or they'll lynch us.' Looking around I could see what he meant: we were literally the only white people in the audience and the rest must all have been high on something as they were in raptures. There we were hanging on to our seats for grim death watching this play which got worse by the minute.

At last Peggy could stand it no longer and she gave a great moan, 'Ooh my back,' she said, and slid off her seat, moaning, 'Ooh, my back, it's gone again!' We all stood up and apologized in whispers to the people around us and helped Peggy to her feet and out to the car park. Well, when we got to the car she recovered miraculously but leant over the bonnet hitting the car with her fists and laughing fit to burst, quoting bits from the 'play'. We got out of the township very quickly and laughed all the way home. Even now when we get together many years afterwards we can still have a giggle at our brush with Native American culture. I'm quite sure that there are excellent companies producing great works all over Canada and certainly mean no disrespect; we just picked the wrong one to see.

Colin's mother was now living in the same area as ourselves having transferred from her flat in inner Bristol to sheltered accommodation in Staple Hill and was only a five minute walk from us. Rosalind, Ken's youngest daughter, and Shona were always visiting her and running errands for her, but she was getting very scatty and being deaf and half blind we worried about her. So when a large house with a granny flat came on the market in our road we asked her if she would like to come and share it with us if we bought it. She was absolutely delighted and so we went ahead and moved – it was only a matter of minutes away from our semi, from number five to number two but a much nicer house. The owner had built it specially so that his parents could share it with them and now the parents were dead and they wanted to downgrade to a smaller house. So we had a very nice house and dear Nell was an excellent neighbour. The people from daycare made sure that she was always included in all the trips organized for the elderly and just about every day she was taken out somewhere. When I came home from school she'd be coming home from a trip and would call me in for a cup of tea. One day I heard her coming in and filling the kettle and then I heard a thumping noise and silence. I rushed in through the interconnecting door and there she was in the kitchen. She still had the kettle in her hand and was lying face down on the floor. Fortunately, the ambulance station was at the end of our road and it only took minutes to have her taken away to hospital. Unfortunately, although she recovered consciousness and lived for a few days, the end had come for dear Nell. I think she knew that she was going although she never said so, but one day, as it happened the last day I saw her alive, she said, 'I'll never forget your kindness to me, I've been so happy living beside you, God bless you and my Colin.'

I'll never forget her either; she was one of a kind. I was at the hospital a few minutes after she died and saw her when the nurses had laid her out. She had a lovely smile on her face, which was wrinkle free and lovely and that is how I shall remember her.

That period in my life was busy as we decided to sell up once again. Shona was at university and the boys had long left home to find their own way in the world. We had one tenant for mum's house but it didn't really work out as she was just in transit after a broken marriage and when her divorce came through she moved to her own flat. We didn't really want anyone else in there. Colin and I were rattling about in two houses which were far too big for us, so without too much hope we put the property up for sale. Well, before the details were printed we had a visit from some people who were moving to the area from outside Bristol and wanted to have their parents living with them. So without further ado we were once again house hunting. It was strange not to have to be near a school for the children as all our property deals up until that time had this clause written in our heads. We had to make our minds up quickly though as our buyer was in a hurry. There was a house up for sale in Bitton, halfway between Bristol and Bath, that I had fancied when we first came to Bristol, but in our fairly penniless state at that time it was way out of our reach. Now with money made from our accelerated romp through the property market and us both earning a good salary we could afford it. So we went to see it and bought it on the spot. High up on a hill overlooking the Avon valley, it was detached and had four bedrooms, so Shona was catered for in her holidays and also the boys in their 'between flats' days. It was a good decision and we were very happy there. There were very nice people living by us and although it was a modern house built on a small estate each house looked away from the other so there was no sense of having to have your make up on first thing in the morning in case next-door was watching. We were the third owners of that house and although it was very nice, one room always seemed cold and dull. We decorated it nicely and always had the heating on but it didn't make any difference. Shona slept there when she was home from university and she also remarked that it was cold. After we'd lived there for some time we learned that the wife of the first owner had lost her baby and had killed herself in that room. From the day we heard the story I kept rosary beads in there and prayed for the poor woman. Perhaps it was my imagination but the room seemed warmer and more welcoming after a while.

My father's health was gradually deteriorating and he was spending more and more time in hospital. I phoned him regularly but after spending a good many minutes on the phone one night he completely threw me by inviting me to come in and have a cup of tea with him if I was in the area and although the house was always full of people and every bed was taken he was sure that his wife could find a space for me. I realized that he did not know who he was talking to and had no idea that he was in the hospital. Poor man, what a dreadful way to end a good life. On one of his 'real life' days he'd told me that he was terrified of the dreadful 'turns' when his lungs seemed to fill up with water and he knew that death was on its way. He said, 'I am not ready to leave you all and I am frightened of what comes next.' We were all very sad when he eventually gave up and went, but at the same time it was a relief that his agony was over. Poor Norman, we still hear his voice often on Gaelic radio but we had lost him some time before he died.

Chapter Eleven

M Y TEACHING YEARS WERE DRAWING to a close as the Special Needs classes were being closed down and all the children were being re-integrated into the mainstream. I don't know which idiot dreamed this idea up, it did not work and now some years later the education departments are re-opening Special Classes under another name and presenting it as a wonderful new idea. I was offered a class in the primary department and was debating whether to take it and carry on teaching or just take early retirement which was also on offer, with a nice bonus payment for all qualified Special Needs teachers. Our headmaster was retiring and a new head was being appointed so I decided to wait and see. Now this sounds like self praise but believe me it is true, my class had become well known for its ability to get children who were 'hopeless' and 'out of control' to toe the line and read, write and do many other things which meant that they were working with the mainstream children most of the time anyway. Teachers from many other schools sent me their children and at least two sets of parents moved house so that their child could attend my Special Needs classes. I feel really embarrassed writing that but any of my fellow teachers from that time could verify it. I can't explain it – I felt a kinship with those children and it was us all together in a race to learn everything the school provided.

So the headmaster who had been at the school for many years left and a female headteacher from an inner London school was appointed. The Bristol educational hierarchy were in a state of turmoil at the time, so many new things were being introduced and they had a lot on their plates. I remember going to a meeting where the director told us all to stop teaching reading, '. . . just give the children lots of books and they will teach themselves.' Well, several of us walked out of the meeting at that stage. There was a major scandal about him a few years later as he had been caught kerb crawling and was sacked but he had the resignations of many good old-fashioned teachers on his conscience.

Meanwhile back at my school there was a lot of trouble going on. I kept away from it as much as I could but as I shared the staff room with the other teachers I could see and hear things I did not like. The new head was very strange. She said that she was a new broom who had come to sweep all the old rubbish away and that our school was going to change drastically. Well, I could see no need for this but like all the rest of the staff was willing to be taught. The school up until then had been chugging along as city schools do, with a staff of good teachers doing their best and the children with brains and application doing well and the rest doing as well as they were able to. We had several after-school clubs, a good music and sports after-school tradition and my own netball team had won the district cup for the first time ever while I was there.

Within weeks of the new head taking over half of the staff were off sick. This was not a fake illness, they were all in various stages of the damage which can be done to your mental capacity by a sadistic attack on everything that you do. Our deputy headmaster was a truly committed teacher who had just recovered from an almost fatal illness when she arrived and questioned his authority on every turn. It was terrible. I used to hate going into school each day to see and hear more of this woman's doings.

Eventually she sent for me and said that she was interviewing the staff one by one as she wanted to appoint a new deputy head and from what she had heard I would make a very good one if I joined the mainstream staff when my class closed. So I asked her what was wrong with our present deputy head and she said, 'Oh, I'm getting rid of him.' I did my best to humour her by saying that I would think about her offer and managed to bring the interview to a safe conclusion. I had already decided that I would take early retirement but didn't want to let her know that.

By now some of the stronger staff who still remained at the school had started putting out feelers about the lady and had found out that she had been very unpopular at her London school as she was half-mad and that she had been having an affair with a student who was there doing teaching practice. To get rid of her, her headmaster had given her a glowing testimonial and that's how she ended up in Bristol. There were several other things that I must not write about in case she ever decides to read this book and takes me to court. However, the staff rebelled and the council suspended the new head, whom I believe gave up teaching which was a good thing too. Unfortunately she had permanently damaged many good teachers and probably blighted the education of the children who were at the school at that time.

Then of course there was the county who could not be seen to have done anything wrong. So they appointed a caretaker headmaster and sent in a posse of advisers recruited, I believe, from out-of-work teachers in a neighbouring county. We had carpets fitted, the library was scrutinised for 'Little Black Sambo' type books and all sorts of political incorrectness was corrected. New teachers were drafted in to replace the ones who had left and the school chugged on. Without me. I finished my term, saw the last of my pupils integrated, took a very handsome additional pension and got the hell out of it.

What sheer and utter bliss it was to drive home the day I finished at that school. I remember singing all the way home! I had lovely memories of my former pupils and many good and steadfast friends to this day among the staff but the last year had not been good. Our ex-headmaster had been vilified by the new head and even his leaving present of a video recorder had been brought into question as having been bought out of school funds. Well, I know that much money had been brought in by the pupils and don't believe for one minute that there was anything wrong with his running of the school or with his leaving present. I hope his retirement was not in any way spoiled by his vile successor, as that he did not deserve.

For many weeks after I left the remaining core of teachers whom I had left behind would come over to the house to visit and tell me of all the new shenanigans at the school as the county tried to cover up their own debacle and the deputy head decided that he had had enough and retired. I believe he now runs a very profitable dog food business. His father was the famous Scottish doctor who discovered the use of chloroform as an anaesthetic and many other things and I'm sure that he must have been turning in his grave when all this was going on.

Gradually the fuss died down and I was having long cycle rides and walking our dog along the Bitton to Bath cycle path, a lovely straight path which had once been a railway but was now a tarmacked path used for dog walking and cycling. You could walk all the way to Bath one way or to Bristol the other way through gorgeous scenery and the cities seemed very far away. Carlo, our King Charles Spaniel, had died a few years before at the ripe old age of fifteen and was much missed by all the family. Mandy, his South African lover girl, who had grown a very thick coat to combat the chill of her new country, took a long time to get over his absence. She used to howl and cry into the sunset every night and looked everywhere for him. So one day, Philip came home from London where he was working with a little puppy as a replacement. It was very cute but turned out to be the dog from hell as it grew up.

Ben was a Staffordshire Bull Terrier and although he was very good looking and had come from a very nice mother his father must have had some evil gene in him as he was bad. From the start Mandy was frightened of him and as he grew up he used to grab her head inside his mouth and run around the garden with her. Then he took to tearing the garden apart, and I mean that in the most literal terms. He would take a piece of grass in his mouth and pull it and in some mysterious way unravel the lawn and leave piles of it all over the garden. Then he discovered that the Anderson carpet in the kitchen could

147

be treated the same way, so there were piles of brown wool everywhere. Colin was busy making a new table for the garden and when he finished it and put it in place he came in full of pride and took me out to see it. Meanwhile Ben had inspected it and had bitten one corner off completely. We put up with it until he started on us. If we told him off he would show no remorse, instead he would growl and advance towards us and I had more than one sharp nip from him. Then one day he bit Colin quite badly and that was the end. We contacted the Bull Terrier Rescue Society and they gave us details of how to get him to them. A palpable sigh of relief was the only sign of his departure. Mandy took his blanket outside and tore it to ribbons and then she once again became the dog she had been before Carlo had died. A few weeks later we had a letter and a photo from a young lady. A photo of two big Bull Terriers and Ben looking angelic. She said that he was settling down well and they were very pleased with him, but did we ever have any trouble with him being destructive as her kitchen table now only had three legs? Well of course, we denied all knowledge. I was sure he'd grow out of his destructive tendencies and hopefully the two older dogs would show him how to treat the human race.

About six months after I retired I had a letter from the county office saying that if I wanted to do supply teaching at any time I was free to do so as I had a few years to go before I was officially of pensionable age and I was allowed to earn quite a decent amount of money yearly before it would affect the pension I was receiving. So I contacted the local school which was a few minutes walk away and as I had had experience of every class in Infant and Junior departments they were delighted. So in no time at all I was back in the classroom again. The difference this time was that the teacher who was off had to leave lessons prepared for me, and all I had to do was show up and teach. It was lovely, a nice school, with reasonably sized classes and if I had something else planned they said, 'Fine, let us know when you are available again.' I had to be very careful not to get sucked back into teaching almost full time and after a few years I told them that I would no longer be available. They were very nice and I am grateful that my final days as a teacher were at such a pleasant school.

Sadly, when she was approaching her thirteenth birthday Mandy left us and we really mourned our little South African smiling dog. So after much consideration I decided to get a West Highland Terrier. I had always loved them but never had the chance to own one and so Harry came. He was a delight in every way. Easy to train and everybody's friend. We were horrified a few months after we got him to find out that he had come from a puppy farm. This is a predominantly Welsh system of making a lot of money by keeping as many as twenty, sometimes more, pedigree bitches locked up in any old byre or shed and breeding them till they are half dead. Then they are either given to the rescue service or shot. So with time on my hands I was determined to redress the grievance in a small way by adopting one of the thrown out bitches. I got in touch with the West Highland Terrier Rescue Service and they gave me the name of Linda Thompson who worked for them in Wales. So we got Mary, a throw out from a puppy farm.

I will never forget that day. Philip was home for a few days and went with us to the Severn Bridge to meet Linda and pick up our new dog. We had been warned that she was in a bit of a state as she had been swarming with lice when Linda received her but she assured us that she was now clean. Well, she had been practically shaved all except her head, which was enormous as her hair had never been cut. And that was full of dead things. There was a big scar just healing up on her head where a mating dog had bitten her so Linda thought it best to wait before cutting her hair. She had killed all the lice and assured us that once the wound had healed the hair could be cut. Her pads were sore as her nails which had never been cut had grown into them and Linda had had the vet in to cut the nails. She assured us that they would heal perfectly well if we kept them clean. The wreckage of a pedigree dog, a testimony to man's inhumanity, and you could just see two black hopeless-looking eyes through the matted hair. Well, even Philip, a shaven-headed kick-boxer had tears in his eyes. When we got home with her Harry was the perfect gentleman. He took her outside and she did her business and we never saw a spot on the floor from day one. She was pathetically eager to please and when we gave her her bowl of food and showed her her nice new basket she made this peculiar flapping sound. We discovered that it was her tail wagging between her legs. We thought she didn't have one as one of the marks of a good Westie is its proud little tail which it always carries aloft, but Mary seemed to have no tail or at least the poor little dog never had the occasion to wave it happily. It took a few months of love and care and as her hair grew and we were able to have her head properly trimmed, she waved her tail with the best of them. She was a beautiful dog. She never got over her delight in being free to wander round the garden and would go up and smell the flowers and wag her tail.

As a way of spending my time now that I had finished work I started to take the dogs up to the local hospital and spent many a day with the old people. They loved to see them and pat them and Mary was always given a special welcome and patted while Harry looked on admiringly. At first we always walked her with a lead as she was very timid and we were afraid that she would run away if a bike or jogger came past her unexpectedly, but after a while we let her run free with Harry and she would come back and walk with us when we called her. We were well pleased with her until, one day, Harry was not very well and he didn't want to go walking so Colin just took Mary and set off along the cycle path as usual. I was surprised to find him running into the house a little while later without the dog and shouting, 'Quick, come and help me, Mary has run away.' It was a pair of roller skaters which had caused her to panic and she put her head down and took off. Colin tried to catch her to no avail. A couple of other walkers were helping him and he had come home to fetch me and my bike to try and speed things up. Well, when I got to the track Mary had gone down the steep incline at the side and had gone into a field full of sheep and lambs. I don't know if she thought they were Westies, but the sheep were very interested in her and were inspecting her without any fear. Colin stayed on the track and I went down the side into the field. Just as I was nearly by her side she took off again up the incline and towards Colin, so we thought that was the end of the escape bid, but no way. She charged past Colin and just kept on running. By this time she had so much mud on her feet that she was about four inches taller than her usual size and her mind was gone. She didn't respond to anything, just kept running. It was incredible. By this time we had many helpers on the track but she evaded us all. Eventually her stamina gave up and she just lay down in front of Colin panting with her eyes shut. We thought that she would die but after a good bath and a sleep she was fine. We kept her on the lead for a long time after that, especially if the rollerbladers were on the track. We had many good days with the two dogs and they went everywhere with us including South Uist, until one day Mary's hard life caught up with her and she laid down and died with no fuss. We missed her sorely, as did Harry.

I was so incensed by the awful puppy farm trade that I sent this poem and Mary's story to a dog magazine and it was printed and copied by many other publications. I fully expected a Welsh backlash but I guess that the Puppy Farmers knew that they were in the wrong and the real Welsh people were as shocked by the situation as anyone else.

VALLEYS OF SHAME

Once there was music in the Land of my Fathers
Songs that could make the old coal miners cry
And I loved to listen to the blend of male voices
As they sang of their homeland, their hills and their
pride.

They're a people so rugged, forged in deep deprivation
And tempered like steel they have fought to survive
Kept their language and culture, a separate nation
As British as Shakespeare but Welsh till they die.

Welsh exiles are hallowed as some of the greatest
Think of Tom Jones and Shirley from far Tiger Bay
There's Sir Anthony Hopkins, and then there is Mary
Her life in the valleys makes the songs go away

Little Mary's a Westie who worked for a farmer
In a place that resembled the darkest of mines

For three thousand days she gave up all her children
Sick and frightened and dirty he threw her aside.

True farmers have honour, they husband their produce
And they tend it with love till it comes to its prime
The earth which has grown it they carefully nurture
With back-breaking labour, till harvesting time.

Farming puppies from bitches kept locked up in cages
Sore, scratching and frightened for years at a time
In dark sheds in great numbers to yield bigger wages
Sucked by pups, fleas and lice and embedded with grime.

So The Land of the Farmers can sing to another
For I'll never recover my love for their songs
As long as they practise the torture of mothers
Who cannot speak up and don't live very long.

Before long we were well into the rescue service and had
helped to home a few more dogs. We had to be very
careful that the right people got the dogs. They did not all
come from puppy farms, some had been given to the
rescue service when an elderly owner died, or had been
abandoned by people who had bought the dog and
discovered that it needed a walk now and again. So then
Linda rang us one day and asked if we would take on
another Westie ourselves as she didn't want to give it to
anyone else; it had been vicious but now it seemed to be
quite normal. She said we could try and see how it
behaved and if it was in any way a problem dog we could
bring it back. We debated it and eventually decided that
we could not refuse. So we got Rosie. She had been at the
rescue kennels for two years. Her owner brought her in
as a pup and said that she was vicious and they couldn't

handle her. Linda had put her in a pen by herself and she had to feed her through the bars for nearly a year for fear of losing her fingers. Then Rosie slowly got less vicious and eventually would beg for her food. She was now at the stage that Linda was even letting her come into the house and she had not shown any vicious tendencies for months. The only problem was that Linda could not deliver the dog as usual as she had trouble with her van, so we agreed to go and get her ourselves.

We went down to Wales to Linda's house to pick the dog up and as we rounded the last corner we saw a large open-topped pen, which appeared to be empty. As we pulled up outside the house the pen erupted. About twenty little white heads appeared bobbing up and down over the top of the pen and the barking had to be heard to be believed. Linda's rescued Westies. There was also another pen where she and her family reared Westies and other dogs and had many prizewinners amongst them. How she found time for the wonderful work she did for the rescue service I shall never know. She brought Rosie in and it was love at first sight for me. This was no vicious dog but a tiny bundle of energy which jumped on our laps and licked us to death. Well, that lasted until last year when, as an ageing lady, she succumbed to an incurable illness and we had to say a sad farewell to her. She was a lovely companion for many years.

The first thing we did after getting Rosie was take her to our own vet for a thorough examination, as we knew that with her busy life Linda only had time to treat the obvious illness that the dogs had before passing them on, and the rest was left to the new owners. Well we all got a shock when the vet told us that she had a blind eye, which had been badly damaged when she was a puppy. In fact he showed us the terrible injuries she had suffered, through a microscope, and her eye, although you couldn't see any difference when looking at it from the outside, was torn to bits on the inside. He said that she must have had a terrible beating as a puppy but was now able to make up for it as everything had healed, but she was totally blind in one eye. Poor little dog, she had probably torn up a cushion or something in her owner's house and he beat her without mercy. That is why she had been vicious and would not let anyone near her until the eye healed up. Poor Rosie.

We lost Harry a few years before Rosie, he had cancer and just gave up one day – a very sad day for us. He was a perfect gentleman and had helped many rescue dogs to become real dogs again. And so then we got Jock, one of Linda's own dogs, who had a curly tail and was ineligible for competitions. She asked us if we wanted him and as Rosie was pining for Harry we thought we would have a companion for her. He is now our only dog and has always been a lovely companion and friend. Rosie bossed him about a lot when he first came to us making him a bit cowed and now that he is on his own he seems to like it. Just as well as we are now getting too old to look after two dogs, but it has been a worthwhile and much rewarding period in our lives.

Colin took early retirement from his job with SERCO and after a rest period started voluntary work with the Citizen's Advice Bureau. Also, we did a few weeks a year at a caravan site on the Isle of Wight as wardens. We got roped into this by friends who did it regularly and it was a nice way of getting a free holiday and getting paid for it. The Isle of Wight is beautiful in the summer and we really enjoyed our time there.

The same friends were cruise fanatics and we went on several lovely holidays with them and saw much of the world from the comfort of a liner. Our first cruise was on the Nile and as there had been some shooting at German cruise ships a few months previously there were hardly any tourists there. Our tour guide assured us that the British flag on our ship would ensure our safety. We visited the Valley of the Kings, passed by Luxor and sailed down to the Aswan Dam. It was wonderful to see houses which have not changed since biblical times with the people waking up in the morning and letting the donkey out.

Then we sailed back and had a glorious week of complete decadence in the best hotel in Luxor. I'll never forget the swimming pool there with men standing by to catch a leaf if it looked like falling anywhere near you!

Our next cruise was to South America and the West Indies where we visited Columbia, the city of Cartagena, Grenada, Trinidad and Tobago and the Leeward Islands. It was also a very good cruise and the entertainment was superb as were the many buffets! Finally we went on a three week New Year cruise starting off at Naples, to Gibraltar, had New Years Eve in Madeira where we anchored in the harbour and watched the wonderful fireworks display and drank champagne to bring the New Year in. Then it was on to the Panama Canal, Jamaica, the Bahamas and Freeport City and finally the Everglades in Florida. Truly wonderful stuff but we would not like to do any more cruising. It would spoil the memories. Our friends do at least three a year. To each his own.

There were also great trips to America where Shona had married and settled and has two lovely little girls called Rose Ellen and Meredith. We visited Canada many times to spend time with Peggy, Colin's sister. Philip had married a nice young Thai lady called Jum, whom he had met in Northern Thailand on one of his many visits there. They live in Oxford with their two sons, Andy and Tom, and we see them frequently. Norman was married twice when he was very young, but neither marriage worked out and he is living a bachelor life also in Oxford.

So our life in Bristol was busy but busy doing the things we liked to do and Colin's large family, mostly cousins now as the dear old aunties had died, were in constant touch. My mother was in Uist House, an excellent place for the old people of the island where they had every good care taken of them and she lived there for many years as did the aunties. We went up from time to time and visited her and stayed at Brae Lynne, which was empty for most of the year. Mary Flora and her husband Ian had moved back to Uist and renovated the old house and were living there so it was always a very enjoyable time. We went to the cemetery and I talked to my father and Chrissie MacIntyre, my friend and neighbour from days of yore, who was in the next plot. The aunties died within a few months of each other, in their mid nineties and are in a plot not a stone's throw from dad. I wonder if Auntie Chirsty still goes on at him about 'My croft'. As the years have gone by there are many more of my dear friends interred in Hallin by the sea than there are left on the island so it never seems like a sad visit.

The changes in the island over the years have been many. As the crofters got more control over their land many new houses were built and there are thriving communities all over the place. Many of the soldiers and teachers and other people who came to the island to work have now made it their permanent home. There is a road going out to Glendale and as far as I know none of the families who lived there in my time are now in residence, but for old times' sake I always go out there for a trip down memory lane. Benbecula too gets the sentimental treatment and I look at the new buildings and pick out the places that have memories for Colin and myself. The army camp is now deserted and for the first time since I was born there is no real military presence in Benbecula. A sign of more peaceful times? Well, let's hope so.

Chapter Twelve

S O LIFE WENT ON AND although we were very happy in
Bristol we had always intended to move back to
Scotland when we retired. But, as it happens with most
people, retirement seems to be as busy as full time work
and you don't realize that you are getting old until it is
too late. We watched as the older aunts and uncles from
our families died and people we worked with moved on,
some to places like France and Italy and others back to
Wales or the North of England, and we carried on as we
were. Our children were well scattered and although they
came to visit from time to time there seemed to be no
point in hoping that they would ever move back to
Bristol. As we had taken them round the world with us in
their young days we could hardly point an accusing
finger at them for wanting to choose their own place. We
had come to Bristol to give our children a place to grow
up in, close to their family and now they were all gone.
And so the search began for a new home, our final
retirement home. We wanted to go back to Scotland,

which had only been a holiday place for me for so many years. Colin had always loved Scotland and he agreed with me that it was now or never. I had followed him without question for all those years and now he was ready for a last move.

We both agreed that to go to Uist would be nice but as our children were a very important part of our lives and it would be very difficult for them to visit us there we started to look at the Scottish Highlands. The property in Kilpheder (my father's croft and two houses) had been split between the three boys and my sister. I was quite happy with that as Colin and I had always been independent. I can't honestly say that any of my children have shown an interest in living in South Uist, so when we're gone they can have what we leave. Anyway, we are always welcome up there and it still feels like home.

As we had both worked with computers at some stage in our lives we had one and used it regularly. So it was easy to look at properties in the North of Scotland whilst drinking a cup of tea in the South of England. Prices had escalated tremendously in our part of the world and we knew that we could sell our house at an immense profit. Scotland had lagged well behind its southern neighbour in the property market so it would be a move which would not harm us financially, even taking into account the cost of having all our goods transported up there.

So the FOR SALE sign went up outside our house in Bitton and we waited for buyers. Our first customer was a man from Bath whose marriage had broken down and he wanted a house for himself and his son. He was very taken with our house and tried to persuade us to take it off the market and keep it for him. There was one drawback: he had not sold his house. So we kept our notice up and sure enough he came back to us to say that he had sold his house but had gone off ours, as it was too big. A few days later a couple came and bought it on the spot. They had sold their house and there were only two other people in the dreaded chain and they seemed fine. Their buyer was a housing association which had agreed to buy and the man had a document from them saying that they were just awaiting the committee meeting where it would all be finalized. The housing association house was being bought by a first time buyer. Great stuff, now all we had to do was rush up to Scotland and buy the house in Roy Bridge, which we had found on the Internet.

We arranged to have our dogs boarded in the local kennels, which we always used if we were going away anywhere, and went up the motorway to Roy Bridge to a hotel which we had found in a tourist guide. We were enchanted by the lovely mountains, and the colours as we drove through the Highlands were breathtaking. We had seen them many times in the past, but looking at them in the knowledge that we were soon to live there was different. Having seen most of the renowned scenery that other countries have to offer we agreed that in Scotland you can find so much more ever-changing beauty within five square miles than you can find in an entire country elsewhere. True, the weather isn't the best in the world, especially in Lochaber, but that is something that we could live with. So we got to Roy Bridge and spent the night at our hotel well pleased. We got the directions for the house, which was walking distance away. It was just what we wanted. There were houses close by but as they each had at least a third-acre plot that wasn't a problem. It was a bungalow. Opposite it was a field with four horses in it and beyond that the River Roy flowed into a meeting with the River Spean. Beautiful mountains on the skyline completed the picture of the place I had always wanted, but on the For Sale sign were the words Under Offer. Obviously the Internet had let us down.

So we spent a few days looking at houses in Fort William and the surrounding district but nothing even came near the place in Roy Bridge. The day before we were due to leave we decided to go and take another look at it and the man next door came out to have a chat. He said that the owners were now living up north and that he had the key if we would like to look inside. We said, 'What's the point, it is already sold.' 'Oh,' he said, 'It is under offer, and that means that if you offer more than the other people then you will get it.' Well, we felt very stupid as we hadn't come into contact with the Scottish system of buying and selling houses before and, needless to say, we were also deliriously happy. When we saw the inside we were delighted with everything, especially the beautiful uninterrupted view of the mountains from the large windows in kitchen and living room. The house had three large bedrooms and was really nice inside. The previous occupant was a builder and had built the house as an investment while working in the area and had lived there with his family for a few years before moving north. The spacious gardens showed signs of neglect as it had been empty for some time, but Colin is a gardening fanatic and I could see him rubbing his hands at the thought of a blank canvas. There was a small wood or coppice of birch trees in the back garden and in the peaceful quiet of a Roy Bridge afternoon all I could hear was the singing of the birds in the trees.

Well, I doubt if a deal had ever been done so quickly before. We got the owner's telephone number from the neighbour, who seemed as excited as we were, and we went to see the estate agent in Fort William straightaway.

I think he thought that we were mad as he asked for ID and Colin, thinking that he was passing him his bank card, gave him his video club card instead. Still, that was soon rectified and the agent said that it was only a matter of days before the time for offers expired and we'd have to move fast. First of all, we had to get back home and get our solicitor to put the offer in for us. We travelled down to England stopping here and there to make phone calls on our mobiles to various people – the agent, the owner, his solicitor, our solicitor – and by the time we got back to Bristol we were shattered but hopeful. About ten days later it was all tied up. The house was ours.

Our buyers were getting very excited and were planning on redecorating and knocking this wall down and putting a new kitchen in etc. etc., so they were in and out of the house all the time. We were very pleased as they really loved the house and the view across the Avon Valley. We were busy packing stuff and had a good firm of removal men coming down from Fort William to take all our belongings to Roy Bridge the day before we left. Yes, every thing was going like clockwork until the removal men had left and we had just come back from a farewell dinner with some friends. There was a frantic phone call from our buyer. The deal was off! The housing association meeting had to be cancelled and his part of the sale would be delayed for at least a month. Well, I hope I never have to go through a time like that evening again! Sitting in an empty house, with our worldly goods halfway to Scotland on the way to a house that we could not buy, don't make me even think of that evening. We phoned the owner of the Scottish house and he seemed very reasonable, saying that we could move in at a very reasonable rent until our own house sold. So we were relieved. Then about half an hour later he called back and said that he'd taken advice and wanted an enormous sum for rent or he would not let the furniture removal men into the house.

By now the evening was gone and we knew that the Scottish solicitors' office would be closed, but fortunately we had his home telephone number so Colin called him and he was most reassuring. He said, 'The owner can't do that, I will call him in the morning and put him straight. Your stuff will be put in the house and you come up and move in. The rent you pay him can be the sum he originally stated to you or it can go to court which will take months, by which time your house deal in England will have gone through.' We were relieved but not happy as it was a situation that was totally new to us. Meanwhile our buyer was in touch again: his wife was hysterical, as she had paid for all the kitchen stuff etc., having measured our rooms, had curtains made and was generally going mad at the thought that it was all for nothing. He had been in touch with the housing association and they assured him that they were definitely buying his house but it would take a little bit longer that they first thought. Armed by this knowledge I phoned the Scottish owner and blasted him for trying to make more money out of our misfortune. It worked and he agreed to go back to our original deal.

I don't ever want to think about that night. Whenever we had moved house before we spent a long time talking about the happy times we had had in the house we were leaving and generally being cheerful, but this time I can honestly say that there was no chitchat just a feeling of dread. In the morning after a sleepless night on bare boards we went to our friends across the way for a lavish breakfast and I could not tell you what we ate. We decided not to tell them about our situation, it was too new to us and still felt a bit awful so we ate and drank and wished them goodbye. As we left the house and drove past they all waved to us and we waved back but at heart we wondered about the wisdom of it all, if we were doing the right thing and what our new country was going to hit us with.

Well, it turned out all right in the end. We met the owner and he was most reasonable and said as he met me, 'God, you frightened the life out of me on the phone! No woman has spoken to me like that before, I'd have agreed to anything!' We all held our breath until two weeks later when we heard from England that the deal had gone through and all the money had been transferred. Big drams all round.

We loved our house and still do. The people are wonderfully friendly and we feel as if we have always lived here. Many of my old friends from my Fort William school days have been in contact and Christine, Florence and Theresa from my class so many years ago join me every Friday for lunch at the Grand Hotel where we talk as if the years of separation had never been. I have met many of my old school friends and even more have written to me after reading my books. It is truly like coming home. We joined the local church soon after arriving here and Father Tom arranged a House Blessing evening here which was very well attended and so we were very quickly integrated into the community. All our children have been here many times. Shona and family even came over from America twice and they are all in agreement that it is a lovely place, as are the English friends who have a sudden desire to see Scotland. We love to see them! We have also re-established our friendship with Dorothy Davidson (Mude) and her husband who have read my first two books in Canada, and have visited us twice. Dorothy was a teacher friend years ago in Daliburgh School and Jean MacDonald (McDonnel) my friend from my carefree days as a young teacher in Uist, who also lives in Canada, has been in touch, as have others from all over the world. I am truly blessed.

Life was good for about six months, and then it all started to go wrong. My young brother, Alick, who lived in Glasgow was taken ill with a lump in his neck and a fast-moving cancer was diagnosed. As he lived alone and I was the closest to him in distance I dropped everything and spent weeks in Glasgow, running between his flat and the hospital. After chemotherapy the doctors told him that he was cured and we all settled down again. Then my eldest brother, Donald Angus, was taken ill – he had been in hospital in London several times with emphysema, but he always seemed to bounce back. Not this time however and he rang me up to say his farewell from the hospital and was dead that night. He was 66 years old and I suppose anyone reading this would say that was a good age, but that is my age now and there is no way I feel ready to go. I was not in any way ready for him to go either. I went down to the funeral and it was a very grand occasion with many members of the AA where he had been a patron for many years giving eulogies. His wife, Sheila, had died some years before but his son and daughter Gordon and Catherine were there and gave their father a wonderful send-off.

A month later young Donald and Alick came to visit us here and we decided that the three of us would go up to Uist to see our mother. We had a lovely time up there and although she had a cold and was not really well she seemed pleased to see us all. The day we were leaving we had the car packed and everything ready for the journey when a phone call came from Uist House to say that

Mum was very ill and could we all go over. Well, we went over and stayed the night by her bed and she died as dawn was breaking. We were thankful that we had gone up there at that time, but heart sore at her leaving us. Although she was ninety-two it is never enough.

I was booked on a pilgrimage to Lourdes as I had heard many tales of the place and the aunties and Mum had been years ago so I thought that I would go and see for myself what the fuss was about. I was also very worried about this dreadful headache I had been having for some time. My left eye was practically blind and I could hardly drive. Doctors had been consulted but despite various examinations the cause was not found. With so much going on in the family I just pushed it all to one side and kept taking more and more tablets to ease the pain. Well, Lourdes was a wonderful experience. We went by coach and although the only people I knew when I left Fort William were Christine Calder and her brother Alistair, by the time we got back we were all like old friends. Father Tom was the priest in charge and he was wonderful. We said prayers and sang the odd hymn on the coach but the camaraderie was great. We stayed at nice hotels and saw much of France on the way there and back. Although the eye was even worse and the pain still there when I got back I was very glad that I had gone. There was a message from Alick when I got back. It was not good news. His cancer had returned and this time it was incurable. So it was up and down to Glasgow again. Donald came up from London regularly and although Mary Flora was busy nursing at the new hospital in Benbecula, she came as often as she could. One day while Alick was in hospital and I was just about to go in with some clean clothes for him I had a phone call from Donald. Gordon, Donald Angus's son had been killed.

He was a pilot and, having just come home to his flat in Brighton, he was having a chat with some friends on the balcony of his flat. He leaned against the railing which collapsed and he fell to the ground. His death was instantaneous and he did not suffer but I still can't believe that it happened. A lovely young man of thirty- three who had everything to live for. I could not go to his funeral as Alick was still in and out of hospital and needed someone to stay with him but I was there in spirit and felt really sorry for poor Catherine who was now the only one of that family left.

Alick died on Boxing Day and was buried in Uist on 2 January. And so ended a year which I like to forget. So many of my loved ones gone and all so close together. I was glad that I had moved to Scotland as I was able to spend some time with Alick and be with my mother the day she died but it is a small consolation. Alick was only fifty-seven and it all seems wrong. However, now that so many of them have gone I no longer fear death as I am sure that we will all be together one day.

Mary Flora was quite badly affected as Alick was her twin and there was always that special bond between them. She wrote this song and Donald has composed a tune for it but I don't have a copy of the music as it hasn't been released yet. However I'm sure she won't mind if I include it:

Alick

Brathair baghail deagh inntinneach,
Eibhinn is cinnteach
Ged nach till thusa tuilleadh
Bi thu riamh faisg rim thaobh
Cha'n eil latha bho'n dh'fhalbh thu

Nach eil thu nam inntinn
Le mis air mo bhrathair
Le gaire 's le gaol.

Fonn:

Thusa Alick diann eisdeachd
Tha thu fhathast mu'n cuairt orm
Fuaim do ghaire nam inntin
Fiamh a ghaire 'nad shuil
Thig an latha mar is corr dhi
A sheasas sinn comhladh
Gu siorraidh mu dhearadh
'N am sheasadh ri d'thaobh.

Ged bu chaomh leat bhi tilleadh
Gu tigh Braigh na Linnidh
Farram ceilidh is sgeulachd
Oidche Shamhraidh cho ciuin
Sinn cruinn uile comhladh
A'cuimhneachadh orain
Do ghuth m'eudail cho milis
Ri binnead cruit chiuil

Bho'n a chaidh sinn air choiseachd
Bha cus tags agam unnad
'S mi leantail a fasgadh
Bha mi faighinn ri d'thaobh
Ged nach till thusa tuilleadh
Chan fhalbh thu as m'inntinn
'Gad chuimhneachadh Alick
Le gaire 's le gaol.

Forever most loyal
Kind, caring and thoughtful

Though you left us forever
You're still close by my side
Every day since you left us
Memories filled with affection
Of you, my dear brother
Live on in my mind.

Chorus:

Now hear me, Alick, and listen
You are still here around me
In my memory your laughter
The smile in your eyes
But a day is a-dawning
When forever and always
For eternal and ever
We'll stand side by side

Loving bonds drew you back
To your home in Brae Lynnie
For long lingering ceilidhs
On a still summers eve'
Family close round together
Minding songs from whenever
Your dear voice always heard
Singing quietly in tune

From our first steps together
You led and I followed
Faithfully and warm from the shelter
That you gave by your side
Though you'll never return
In my mind you're here with me

For you my love and affection
Lives on for all time

Gaelic and English version composed by Mary Flora
Forrester, (Mac Millan) South Uist, January 2005.

All through their lives Alick and Mary Flora were very
close. I never heard them have a cross word and my grief
at his passing must be very minor in comparison to that
suffered by his twin.

My headaches were getting worse and my left eye was
blind but the doctors had given up trying to find the
cause. I had a letter from Inverness Hospital asking me to
attend a meeting with a doctor who was writing a paper
on unexplained illnesses and I dutifully went there. The
doctor did not turn up as he had to go somewhere else so
another doctor took me into a room and had a good look
at my eye. He called another one, who had been examining me before, and said, 'Look at this.' He had found the
cause of my trouble. I had a CT scan, two MRI scans and
an angiogram, which revealed a large aneurysm pressing
on the optic nerve for the left eye and causing the
blindness. The doctor said that it was starting to affect
the other eye and was in danger of bursting which could
mean death. I hardly had time to pack as a bed was found
for me in Aberdeen immediately. As Father Tom came
and gave me the last rites I broke down and cried quietly
for Colin, whom I thought I thought I was leaving
forever. I was taken into hospital very quickly and
although the doctors and nurses were very nice there was
absolutely nobody that I knew living in Aberdeen so the
two days while I waited for the operation were very
boring and I just wished the time away. Colin came in to
see me but we had agreed that he would go home in a few

days and get the dogs settled back, keep the home fires burning and wait for me at home. He flatly refused to leave before the operation and was doing his best to keep his own and my spirits up. Strangely enough I was quite calm but I suppose that being high on drugs helped. The room was an acute ward for people with brain operations either waiting like me or in various stages of recovery and was always very busy. I had so many cards and bouquets of flowers delivered that they had to pass some of the flowers on to the next ward, and so many phone calls that the nurse gave me my own mobile extension. Thank you all and I apologise if I sounded slightly drunk: the tablets have that effect!

I had many phone calls from the children and for the first time in my life I longed to be like all the other mothers whose families came to see them every day. Then on the second day I went outside to wait for Colin coming in and I saw him in the distance but in front of him was someone else. With a broad smile on his face carrying flowers and another package was Philip. It took me a few minutes to recognize him as I thought he was at university in Bristol doing an exam. What a lovely surprise that was. He spent the day with me and his gift of designer perfume and other lovely things was wonderful. He had to make a few phone calls to re-schedule his exam but he'll never know how good it was to see him.

Well, the next day I had a six-hour operation, which was a complete success. My sight returned and I have not had a headache since. The days after the operation I was a bit of a non-person but gradually came back and one day I came out of my drugged sleep to find Mary Dalzell (Boyle) my college friend from Ireland sitting by my bed. I probably talked absolute drivel all the time she was there but, Mary, I really appreciated the long journey you made to come and see me. As I got better I mounted a campaign to get home and my surgeon the marvellous Mr Currie promised to do what he could. He called in to see me at least once a day and brought another surgeon, Mr Binnie who had read my books and had been up to Kilpheder to see the house. A couple of days before I left the hospital my neighbour, Mary Mac Donald, from Kilpheder came in with her daughter who lives in Aberdeen, very close to the hospital. Her daughter had been home for a holiday and Mary had come out to her house where she spends most of the winter. It was a great visit and they came back the next day again. People are so kind. Needless to say the operation takes a long time to get over but I am within weeks of the two year recovery period and although my memory is not as good as it used to be and I have a weakness in my left side the alternative is much more frightening. Was it the trip to Lourdes that saved me? I wonder.

I do know that I was near death, as the last few weeks before the operation are a complete blur. Shona and her daughters came over from America and Norman, Philip, Jum and the two sons all came and spent time here while she was at home but I can't remember a thing about it, just the occasional flash of memory comes back now and again, yet I cooked and talked and went places with them. Believe me it was frightening and to be sitting here typing is a marvellous thing. I was in hospital in Aberdeen for two weeks and a bit and then in a convalescent home in Fort William for three days. I kept asking to go home and in the end they let me. Colin was the best nurse of all. He got me back to normal in no time. Colin and the beautiful mountains that I see every day, a picture in summer and winter.

Chapter Thirteen

NOW THE TIME HAS COME to put the computer away and enjoy the rest of my life, which has been given to me by the doctors and by the gift of God. Don't worry, I am not going to become a boring preacher, it was never my style. I will now however treat every day as a bonus, and my life as one to celebrate. At least that should be my intention, we'll see how long it lasts. Things still annoy me and I get ratty at times, but that's human nature.

There are people not too far away from me who still have the idea that if you have a Hebridean accent you are stupid. Not too long ago I came across this when a doctor was examining my eye in Fort William. He said, 'I can't find a thing wrong with you, my dear. You go back on the boat and we'll send for you next year.' Well, it wasn't just his words but the fake Hebridean accent he used that made me so mad that I had to wait a few minutes before I blasted him. I told him that there is no boat from Roy Bridge; and that I had lived in places he could only dream of and had worked very hard to keep my lovely Highland accent although I had not lived up there for forty years; that it is an accent admired the world over and that's more than he could say about his Glasgow twang. Well, he apologized and the little nurse who was helping him was in stitches, but it made me so angry! '*Chan eil mis air fathiche na dhuthaich fhein,*' as they say. 'A prophet is not honoured in his own land.' Believe me, Islanders, your accent is to be proud of and don't let any ignorant Lowlander tell you otherwise.

There is always plenty to do here and the garden is now very much a pleasure. Colin has been busy and the train slows down when the daffodils are out so that the Japanese tourists can take pictures of the wood and the many lovely bulbs blooming around it. Our friends, Colin and Sylvia, have an immaculate half-acre and are very generous with cuttings, so Colin is happy.

I have seen all I want to see of the world. Glen Spean Park in Roy Bridge is now to me the best place there is. I have been very fortunate in liking every place in which I lived but have always been willing to go and see a new place. Perhaps I have my parents to thank for that, launching me off on my own with tales of what a great life I was going to have with the dear old aunties who raised me to the best of their ability in Benbecula and Barra, who knows. It certainly helped my knack for storing happy times in my mind. I am fortunate indeed for having been given the English soldier to make every new place an adventure.

So now, as my health improves and I get older and wiser (I hope), I have little more to say. I have been so lucky to have been born and bred in the islands and to have been able to come back within visiting distance of them again:

Mo mhile beannachd aig an t-shluagh
Tha'n Uibhist, tir mo ghraidh.

A thousand blessings on the folk
In Uist, land of my love.